Fifty More
Great
Pub
Crawls

EDITED BY BARRIE PEPPER

CAMRA

BOOKS

Published by CAMRA, The Campaign for Real Ale,
230 Hatfield Road, St Albans, Hertfordshire AL1 4LW
T 01727 867201
F 01727 867670
E camra@camra.org.uk
www.camra.org.uk

First published 2003

Printed in the United Kingdom at
the University Press, Cambridge

Design/typography: Dale Tomlinson
Fonts: The Antiqua & Taz (lucasfonts.com)
Copy-editing: Kate Green
Maps: David Perrott
Illustrations: Christine Jopling
Cover design: Rob Howells

ISBN 1 85249 175 2

*Every effort has gone into researching the contents of
this book, but no responsibility can be taken for errors.*

Introduction

ANYONE WHO READ THE PREDECESSOR to this book, *Fifty Great Pub Crawls,* may remember that in it I attempted to define a pub crawl and I gave some of the history of this pleasurable activity. I wrote:

> *'The fine art of pub crawling is to work out a route which allows you to visit a number of pubs, all selling good beers and, ideally, of some character and interest. And even better that the crawl should start and finish close to the same point and near to good public transport connections.'*

Nothing has changed since then except to say that in the four years since the last guide I have found that drinkers are demanding a much greater reliance on public transport. This is wholly to be commended. Twelve of the crawls in this new guide require that either trains, trams, buses and in one case a water taxi be used. And most of the others have start and finish points at railway and bus stations.

Another change in this guide is to include crawls in major cities on the continent. As the world becomes smaller it is often cheaper for someone like me living in Leeds for example to spend a weekend in, say, Amsterdam or Brussels than one in Aberdeen or Plymouth. And getting there is probably quicker. This implies no disrespect to those two fine cities – check out crawl number one in *Fifty Great Pub Crawls* and the Plymouth entry in this book.

So there is an even greater variety and wider geographic spread than before. There are crawls around cities, market towns and villages; you can choose a country walk or a ramble; take a train ride or hop on and off a bus or a tram, or even buy some bottles from the off-licence and settle down at home and take a virtual pub crawl. It's up to you. Occasionally you may find an entry in ***red italic type*** which means that the pub is in the 'try also' category – if you have time, call in, otherwise pass by and your crawl will be no worse for having missed it out. And if you fancy a few days away on a pub crawl holiday then you will find this has all been worked out for you with several grouped together in popular locations.

Thanks are due

To the following CAMRA members and branches for helping to compile this book either by suggesting and in several cases drafting a crawl, preparing one to my brief, or by taking photographs and drawing maps: John Ashton, Mark Ashton, Phil Ayling, Yvette Bacon, Andrea Briers, Phil Clark, Dave Cunningham, Brian Davies, Rod Davis, Graham Donning, John Duce, Peter Dyer, Trevor Edwards, Mary Galliers, Kate Green, Roger Hall, Tim Hockenhull, Melvyn Huntley, Keith Jackson, Jon le Sueur, Simon Linford, Nigel Mullinder, William Ottaway, Ken Parr, David Pepper, Richard Putley, Alan Risdon, Phil Rogers, Gordon Small, Bob Steel, Geoff Strawbridge, Jack Thompson, Guy Thornton, Colin Valentine, Bob Wallis, Terry Walsh, John White.

Abercolwyn, Canterbury, Herne Bay and Whitstable, Colchester and North East Essex, Cornwall, Croydon and Sutton, Edinburgh and South East Scotland, East and Mid Surrey, East Dorset, Furness, Hull and East Yorkshire, Kingston and Leatherhead, Newark-on-Trent, North Manchester, Shrewsbury and West Shropshire, South West London, Stafford Stone and Central Staffordshire, Swansea, Wakefield, West Lancashire, Westmorland, West Norfolk, Worcester.

If any member or branch has been missed out then please accept my sincere apologies.

Special thanks go to Christine Jopling for the wonderful illustrations, Ted Bruning for providing three London crawls and bags of support, Mick Slaughter for two crawls and lots of patience, Dale Tomlinson for the layout and keeping his sense of humour, David Perrott for the maps, Rob Howells for the cover, Mark Webb for starting the whole thing off and Carolynne for listening to me going on and on and on and still driving me to the pub – and back again.

BARRIE PEPPER

DESPITE THE FACT that the Lake District in the north-west of England is quite compact, being just 30 miles from north to south and 25 miles across, it is the largest and without doubt the most popular of the national parks in England and Wales. Within it is a remarkable collection of lakes and mountains, including England's largest lake and highest mountain. It has been an amazingly popular tourist area since the railways reached the area in the Victorian era. You can add to its scenic and sporting properties some important historic sites, eminent literary associations and an assembly of inns, pubs, taverns and hotels that will hold its own with any similar grouping in the nation.

Some of the pub crawls included in this section of the guide are based on the use of public transport and useful information is given in the detail of each crawl.

Cumbria/Lake District

Ambleside

THE LAKE DISTRICT is one of the wettest places in Britain. It is also often crowded beyond comfortable limits. So how can its popularity be explained? One reason is that there is certainly no shortage of good pubs mostly scattered around in the same haphazard way as the lakes and mountains of the area. But, occasionally, you come across a collection, a covey, a concordat, even a crawl of fine pubs in one place. So it is with Ambleside at the north end of Lake Windermere. This popular resort is famous as a centre for fell walking and mountain climbing, for sheep dog trials and its literary associations with William Wordsworth and Beatrix Potter. There is a good bus service linking the town with Windermere, Grasmere and Keswick and ferry services run to it on the lake from Bowness.

Start at the **Golden Rule** (1) at the north end of the town in Smithy Brow, just off the Kirkstone road. First of all, if the season is right, admire the window boxes which win many prizes. This is a very homely three-roomed pub which does not have a juke box or a pool table but does have lots of interesting pictures on the walls and plenty of conversation. The choice of beers is from the Robinson portfolio: **Robinson's Hatters**, **Best Bitter** and **Frederics** and recognising its former ownership **Hartleys XB** and a seasonal special. Meals as such are not served but you can buy well-filled sandwiches and pork pies. The eponymous Golden Rule is a brass measuring yard mounted above the bar.

Go towards the town centre and Smithy Brow links into North Road and on the right is the **Unicorn Inn** (2), a real old world inn with original oak beams and a log fire. It has an excellent bar food menu and a comprehensive wine list. This is another Robinson's pub with **Old Stockport**, **Frederics**, **Hartleys XB** and a seasonal special on the hand pulls. There are occasional jazz sessions. Bed and breakfast accommodation is available here (015394 33216).

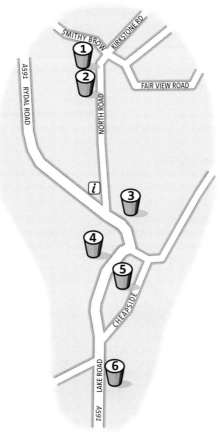

Ambleside

Continue in the same direction and on the left of the Market Place is the **Salutation Hotel** (3) (015394 32244) with a comfortable public bar that serves **Theakston XB** and bar food all day. There is a separate dining room. Dogs are allowed in the hotel bedrooms.

Also in the Market Place is the **Queen's Hotel** (4) another busy residential hotel with a public bar (015394 32206). There is a fine range of ales on offer with **Black Sheep Best**

Bitter, **Tetley Bitter**, **Coniston Bluebird**, **Jennings Cumberland Ale** and **Jennings Bitter** often on the hand pulls but the beers change regularly. This is a popular bar with snacks available up to 6 pm. There are two restaurants which open all day into the evening and both are no-smoking. There is an agreeable patio at the rear sheltered by a large tree but beware of the birds.

And before leaving the Market Place visit the **White Lion** (5) a busy two-bar pub selling **Draught Bass** and **Worthington's Bitter**. There is no juke box and a separate no-smoking area. Food is served all day at the weekend with barbecues if the weather permits.

Some 200 yards along Lake Road is the **Royal Oak** (6) a small two-roomed pub with an open fire in the back bar. Here again there is no canned music but a warm, welcoming atmosphere. **Theakston Best Bitter** is a regular beer and guests may include those from local micros or come from as far afield as **Brains** in Cardiff. It opens all day in summer and serves snacks.

Into the Lakes by rail

LETTING THE TRAIN take the strain is an excellent way of visiting some of the best pubs in the Lake District. This crawl starts at Oxenholme, a suburb of Kendal, and a station on the west coast main line from Euston to Glasgow at its junction with the branch line to Windermere. There is also a through service from Manchester Airport. At each of the five stations there is a chosen pub within a quarter of a mile although others are mentioned and, in particular, you are offered a visit to the pub that has won more awards than any other in the Lakes. What is more this is a very family-friendly pub crawl with most of the pubs welcoming families during reasonable hours.

The station treats itself to the full description of 'Oxenholme – The Lake District'. Leave from the southbound platform, go up the approach road, turn left, and head up the B6254. There is a paved footpath until just short of the top of the hill. From that point on you share the road with traffic so take care. And suddenly, there, at the T-junction with the Sedbergh road, is the **Station Inn** (1) (01539 724094) a neat and well-appointed two-roomed place that does a brisk trade in meals in its family conservatory. At the bar four cask-conditioned beers are on sale: **Boddingtons Bitter**, **Theakston Bitter** and **Flowers Original** plus a guest beer. There is a small outdoor area for summer drinking. Retrace your steps to the station and catch a Windermere train to the next stop at Kendal. This is an hourly service with trains leaving at around half past the hour and taking about 20 minutes to do the full journey to Windermere.

Alight at Kendal and turn right out of the station, go under the bridge, then left into Ann Street and right to Castle Street for the **Castle Inn** (2) (01539 729983). This long, low, stone-built pub is quite popular selling **Jennings Bitter**, **Tetley Bitter** and guest ales with one of them usually from the **Dent Brewery**. The food here, served at lunchtimes, is

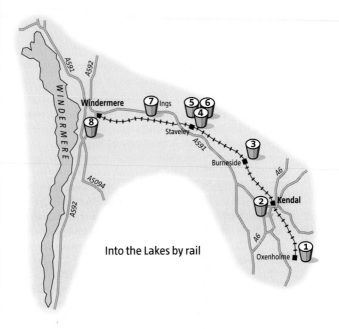

Into the Lakes by rail

extremely good value with a wide range. Note the framed windows from the former Dutton Brewery of Blackburn. There is bed and breakfast accommodation.

Other pubs nearby which are worth a visit are the *Prince of Wales Feathers* and the *Victoria Tavern*. Allow yourself a few extra minutes to return to the station. It is not far away but there is a busy road to cross and a final huffing, puffing slope up to the station. Next stop is Burneside which is a request stop so make sure you let the conductor know you want to get off there.

Alight at the single platform, go out through the level crossing gate, down a few yards of approach road and then right, past the church on the left and the post office to the next call, the **Jolly Anglers** (3) (01539 732552). The pub dates back to 1650 and today sells **Theakston Best Bitter** and a guest beer. There is a comfortable main bar and a no-smoking dining room. Accommodation is available here and there is live music at weekends. Go back to the station for the next train to Staveley. At unmanned halts such as this you need to make your signal clear to the driver of the oncoming train.

At Staveley leave the platform, go down the steps, and ahead at the nearest end of a terrace of houses is Number one, The Banks, better known as the **Railway Inn** (4) (01539 821385). It has a pleasant, cottage feel about it – typical of many Lakeland pubs. To the right is a no-smoking function room, while the bar counter area contains space set aside for diners. There is also a large open fire in a fine surround that is most cosy and welcoming. Beers on draught include **Tetley Dark Mild** and **Bitter** and **Marston's Pedigree** but the menu often changes. Food is available at most sessions and there is bed and breakfast accommodation. There is live music at weekends. Fishing permits can be obtained here. This is the nearest pub to the station but a visit to the *Good Beer Guide* listed **Eagle and Child** (5) (01539 821320) in Kendal Road is worth while if you have time. It is a pleasantly refurbished Victorian inn with a range of beers mainly from local micros. It has two gardens: a secluded one behind the pub and another across the road alongside the River Kent. It does lunchtime and evening meals and accommodation is available. The *Duke William* (6) is also worth a visit and the three pubs in themselves make a mini pub crawl.

The next stop by train is the terminus at Windermere but for those who are prepared to take a four-mile walk instead there is the opportunity to visit one of the Lake District's best-known and best-loved pubs. Go into the village and turn left down to the main Kendal to Windermere road (A591). An alternative is to use the frequent Cumberland bus service No 555.

It is about two miles to Ings and after the petrol station turn left and just beyond the church is the **Watermill Inn** (7) (01539 821309) which backs on to the River Gowan. There are two bars, one that accepts families and the other welcomes dogs with a bowl of water and a biscuit. The food is imaginative and excellent and is served most of the day. The remarkable range of 16 cask-conditioned beers, which always includes several from local breweries, can be viewed

through a glass wall in the ground floor cellar. There are also many foreign beers on draught and in bottle. Seven en-suite bedrooms are available in this family-run pub that was once a water-powered wood mill. And, just for the record, there are no juke boxes, fruit machines or other disturbing contraptions. The pub, a *Good Beer Guide* regular, opens all day.

In September of each year the villages of Staveley and Ings jointly promote the Lakeland Festival of Storytelling and events are held in several of the pubs. Further information can be obtained from Taffy Thomas on 01539 435641.

It is a further two miles along the main road to Windermere Station either on foot or by bus.

Go down the hill from the railway station to Cross Street and the **Elleray Hotel** (8) (01539 443120). There are two bars, a no-nonsense public with pool and machines and a comfortable lounge with a real fire. The beer range varies but usually includes one from a local brewery. The dining room is no-smoking, accommodation is available and occasionally there is live music.

There are several other pubs and hotels selling real ales in the town – the *Grey Walls* is worth a visit – and the more adventurous may choose to walk down the long hill to Bowness and Lake Windermere to find several more, often with local Cumbrian ales on the bars.

Northern Lakes by bus

THIS IS A DIY CRAWL from Penrith to Keswick or the other way round if you wish. Stops can be left out to suit your own timings. A leaflet published by the Stagecoach bus company in cooperation with CAMRA gives bus times and some scanty pub information from Penrith to Keswick, Cockermouth and Workington. The chosen section for this crawl contains fuller descriptions of the pubs but it does not rule out extending it beyond Keswick. However the leaflet certainly helps with its timetables and copies can be obtained by phoning Traveline Cumbria on 0870 608 2608. Without going into too much detail there are half-hourly services on the X4, X5 and X50 routes up to 6.20 pm and three later buses with the last return from Keswick at 9.50 pm. On Sunday the service is cut down to two-hourly with a last bus back at 6.45 pm.

Penrith bus station is in the town centre and the first stop on our route is at the railway station which is on the west coast main line from Euston to Glasgow.

Walk from the railway station down Ullswater Road and across the roundabout in Castlegate is the **Agricultural Hotel** (1) a former entry in the *Good Beer Guide* that is known locally as the 'Aggie'. A full range of **Jennings** beers and 25 malt whiskies are sold along with excellent home-cooked meals at lunchtimes and in the evenings. The pub opens all day.

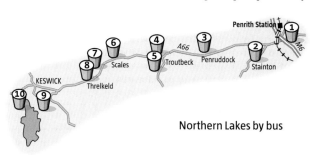

Northern Lakes by bus

It is comfortable and busy with a cosmopolitan mix of customers. A log fire adds to its charm. Bed and breakfast is available (01768 862622).

The next stop is Stainton but only the X50 services call here, although there are a few others on route 105, best to check. In the village is the **King's Arms** (2) where you will find **Castle Eden Ale**, **Tetley Bitter** and guest beers in summer. The pub closes in the afternoons and good bar food is available at all sessions. The pub has been well refurbished without trying too hard to look old-fashioned. There are pleasant outdoor drinking areas.

Move on to Penruddock a quiet village under the fells for the **Herdwick Inn** (3). This 18th-century inn once called the Norfolk Arms, sells **Theakston Best Bitter** and has an excellent restaurant. The bar closes in the afternoons. There are five letting bedrooms (017684 83007).

You could miss out on the next pub – the *Sportsman Inn* (4) at Springfield near Troutbeck – for two reasons. It is rather isolated and it sells **Jennings** beers which are all too readily available in this area. However its reputation for good food with excellent all day bar snacks is well appreciated.

A mile down the A66 is the **Troutbeck Inn** (5) in the eponymous village. This also sells **Jennings Cumberland Ale** and **Draught Bass** as well and the range varies occasionally. There are two bars with real fires and a dining room. Bed and breakfast and self catering is available (017684 83635). It closes during afternoons and lunchtimes during the week in winter.

It is a short run to Scales and the **White Horse Inn** (6) at the foot of Blencathra and on the coast to coast cycle trail. Walkers are made very welcome. **Black Sheep Best Bitter**, **Jennings Bitter** and occasional guest beers are on the hand pulls in this former coaching house. There are real fires and no juke box, machines or TV and whilst the emphasis is on food this is a very comfortable pub. It opens all day.

The penultimate stop is Threlkeld, a pretty village with the Cumbrian hills as a backdrop and an interesting mining museum. At the bus stop is the **Horse and Farrier** (7) a 17th-century inn that has been modernised and is geared towards food. However, **Jennings Bitter**, **Cumberland Ale** and

Sneck Lifter along with the brewery's seasonal ales are on the bar. Bed and breakfast is available (01767 79688).

Nearby is the **Salutation** (8), this is another pub that welcomes walkers with, in particular, a roaring log fire. The beers are mainly from the Scottish and Newcastle range and can include **Courage Directors**, **Greene King Ruddles Best**, **Theakston Mild**, **Best Bitter** and **Old Peculier**. There is bar food at lunchtimes and in the evenings and the pub is very child-friendly. There is no accommodation but the licensees have two self-catering cottages in the village (01767 79614).

The longest stretch of the route follows – a ten-minute run over the five miles into Keswick. This is the capital of northern Lakeland, a pretty town situated under the handsome fells and close to beautiful Derwentwater. Tourism is its main industry and this shows unfortunately in its pubs. There is very little wrong with the pubs but the choice of beers is so limited as to be almost non-existent. It is either Jennings or Theakston and little else. It is worth spending some time here – there are three interesting museums and it is a good town for eating. Two pubs have been chosen – one because it is the nearest to the bus station and is interesting, and the other because it is the choice of the local branch of CAMRA for the *Good Beer Guide*.

Walk down from the bus station to Main Street, turn right, and 100 yards along is the **Bank Tavern** (9), a **Jennings** house selling **Dark Mild** (quite rare this beer), **Bitter**, **Cumberland Ale**, **Sneck Lifter** and seasonal specials. It opens all day and serves an extensive lunch and evening menu. It is one of the oldest pubs in town and has no juke box or TV; bed and breakfast is available (01767 72663).

Continue down Main Street and at the fork of Lake Road is the **Dog and Gun** (10) selling **Theakston Best Bitter** and **Old Peculier**, **Yates Bitter** and guest beers from Easter. The pub opens all day and good value food is served up to 9 pm. There are two bar areas, one stone-flagged and the other with high-backed settles. The collection of local photographs is particularly outstanding.

With two exceptions, the rest of the pubs in Keswick selling traditional beers are within 50 yards of the two mentioned here, and you will have already passed most of them.

South Lakes ramble

THIS WALK, through some of the most attractive parkland, woodland and coastal scenery in the Lakes, is eight miles long or there is a shortened version of just three miles. Both are circular treks. The use of Ordnance Survey Outdoor Leisure map 6 – The English Lakes, South Western Area, or Touring Map 3 – Lake District is highly recommended.

The walk starts at Foxfield which is well served by train and bus and is the home of the Prince of Wales pub and the associated Foxfield Brewery. You could, I suppose, have a quick one here before starting the ramble but most folk will leave this pleasure until the end.

Turn right down the road for 200 yards to a signpost for the Cumbria Coastal Way up to your left. Follow this track upwards, passing through two gates to a farm on your left and 100 yards past here go with another coastal way sign on your left. (An alternative is to carry on down the lane to the main road, turn left and follow this to Broughton Square and meet up with the main route.) At the bottom of a walled field a footbridge can be sighted to your right. The path to this can be boggy after heavy rain. Cross the footbridge and go up the banking to your right on to the Eccles Rigg golf course. Head for the small wood which is 200 yards ahead on your right. An entrance to the wood is found through a kissing gate and within a few steps you emerge into a small hamlet. Turn right and follow the road all the way until you arrive on the outskirts of Broughton-in-Furness. Turn left and follow the main road down into the square.

Here is your first stop at the **Manor Arms** (1). This 18th-century free house has a comfortable, relaxed atmosphere even when busy. It stocks up to seven real ales including **Coniston Bluebird**, **Taylor Best Bitter**, **Yates Bitter** and guests along with **Liefmans Kriek** on draught and several continental bottled beers – a mini beer festival at all times. It is noted for good sandwiches and accommodation is

South Lakes ramble

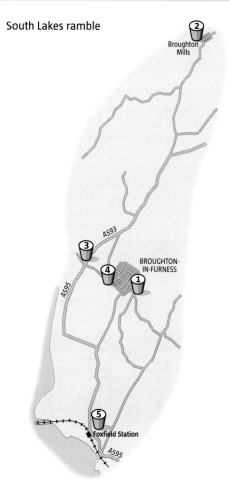

available (01229 716286). The short crawl takes in number 3 and 4 pubs in reverse and misses out the Blacksmiths Arms.

Leave the Manor and head straight up the road past the teashop on the corner. Go along the road for about a mile until you reach a track on your left opposite some large iron gates. Take this track towards Manor Farm skirting the farm on your left. Keep along the path until reaching a stile on the left at the bottom of the rise. Go through the stile and head for and cross the footbridge in the middle of the field. Then follow the path up to Lower Bleansley Farm. From the farm take the road to the right for about a mile until a turn off to the right appears and follow this road towards Hartley Ground until you reach the top of the hill – a farm is on your left. At the junction turn left and follow the road down to the second stop.

The 300-year-old **Blacksmiths Arms** (2) at Broughton Mills, a superbly peaceful little hamlet, is a classic unspoilt pub with hanging baskets and tubs of flowers at the front in summer. There are four rooms all simply furnished and with slate floors and open fires in three of them and a pleasant outdoor drinking area. The bar has an ancient range and a large scrubbed table and there is a choice of **Jennings** beers and guest beers often from local micro-breweries, interesting bottled beers and farm cider.

It opens all day and food is served in the other three rooms, one of which is no-smoking. There are no machines or piped music – instead you will find darts, cards, dominoes and books and games for children. The pub is on the CAMRA National Inventory.

There are various ways back to Broughton using footpaths as the OS maps will show but for those unfamiliar with the area the road can be taken. Leave the Blacksmiths and head up the hill until you meet the junction with the main road between Torver and Broughton. Turn right on to the A593 and follow the road until you reach a junction with the A595 sign posted Workington. Take this road and after a few hundred yards you arrive at the **High Cross** (3), which although mainly an eating establishment has a good selection of real ales with usually four or five to choose from and excellent views over the Duddon valley. **Marston's Pedigree** and **Theakston Best Bitter** and guest beers are usually available. It opens all day and food is served at lunchtimes and evenings. There is no juke box. Bed and breakfast is available (01229 716272).

Leave the pub and turn left down the hill to Broughton. At the bottom on the right is the **King's Head** (4), a 17th-century former coaching inn with friendly, obliging service and **Boddingtons Bitter**, **Castle Eden Ale** and **Hartleys XB** on the hand pulls. There is a separate games area, a small, cosy no-smoking restaurant and tables outside in good weather. Accommodation is provided in comfortable, spacious bedrooms (01229 716293). It opens all day.

Leaving the King's Head stroll back into Broughton Square and walk past the Manor until you reach a signpost for Foxfield pointing to the right. Follow this road down to the junction with the A595 and turn left heading towards your final destination the **Prince of Wales** (5) and the **Foxfield Brewery**. The pub is comfortable and offers a wide, varied range of beers including some of its own and one from its twin, the **Tigertops Brewery** in Wakefield, and always a mild. There is usually a foreign beer on tap and a selection of European bottled beers. It opens Wednesdays and Thursdays from 5 pm to 11 pm and all day from Fridays to Sundays. The food is all home made and is exceptionally good. Newspapers and magazines are provided and bed and breakfast is available (01229 716238).

Travel Information
Buses run to Foxfield and Broughton from Ulverston, Barrow-in-Furness and Millom. For details contact Traveline on 0870 608 2608
Trains to Foxfield from the south come via Barrow-in-Furness or from the north via Millom. There are no trains on Sundays.
For details contact National Rail Enquiries on 08457 48 49 50
A local weather forecast can be obtained on 017687 75757.

Into the Lakes by stagecoach

THE AFTERNOON was not cheerful but it did not rain till we came near Windermere. I am always glad to see Staveley; it is a place I dearly love to think of – the first mountain village that I came to with William when we first began our pilgrimage together. Here we drank a bason of milk at a publick house, and here I washed my feet in the brook, and put on a pair of silk stockings by William's advice. Nothing particular occurred till we reached Ings chapel. The door was open, and we went in. It is a neat little place, with a marble floor and marble communion table, with a painting over it of the last supper, and Moses and Aaron on each side. The woman told us that "they had painted them as near as they could by the dresses as they are described in the Bible", and gay enough they are. The marble had been sent by Richard Bateman from Leghorn. The woman told us that a man had been at her house a few days before, who told her he had helped to bring it down the Red Sea, and she had believed him gladly! It rained very hard when we reached Windermere.

From *Lakeland Journals* by Dorothy Wordsworth

IF ANY PART OF THIS LAND can be called unspoilt it is East Anglia. A story is told that an American film producer asked the press office of the Brewers Society to point him to an inn unchanged since the 1930s. 'Go to any Adnams pub,' he was told, 'and ask them to take out the lager font.' It is known as the grain basket of England for the quality of the barley grown, much of which is malted for use in brewing. There are upwards of 50 regional and micro-breweries here.

Here are the flatlands, the broads, the fens of Cambridge, the beaches of Norfolk and Suffolk and the contrasting features of Essex ranging from its industrial links with London to the brash coastal resorts. Ancient churches poke their spires high above their homely townships and with stately homes they welcome visitors. Steam trains abound.

It was an area that suffered most from the rape of regional breweries in the fifties and sixties when predators such as Watney Mann bought up local breweries, closed them and pumped their tasteless keg beers into the pubs. Now all has changed and today there are scores of splendid inns in Eastern England serving many fine traditional ales.

Colchester

Colchester is ... large, very populous; the streets fair and beautiful; there are abundance of very good and well built homes.
DANIEL DEFOE *A Tour Through the Whole Island*

COLCHESTER was the first city to be founded by the Romans although folk had lived here for a millennium before that. It is rich in Roman and later remains, including a large Roman gate and the high adjoining walls, built after Queen Boudicca and the Iceni burnt the town down in AD 60 when she failed to oust the Romans.

From Colchester Town Station take the path heading anticlockwise at the roundabout to enter St Botolph's Street. As you head up the hill it becomes Queen Street where those using the bus station will join the route. At the top of Queen Street on the right is the Tourist Information Centre, whilst in front the impressive Norman castle comes into view. The castle is well worth a visit with exhibits showing Colchester's Roman past and its involvement in the Siege of Colchester during the English Civil War. Turn left up the High Street where the clock tower of the Victorian town hall soon dominates the skyline, along with the huge water tower affectionately known as Jumbo.

Turn right by the town hall to descend West Stockwell Street, also famous as the home of the Taylor sisters who wrote the nursery rhyme Twinkle, Twinkle Little Star. The **Stockwell Arms** (1) is at the bottom of the hill on the right. Situated in the town's historic Dutch Quarter, this timber-framed building dates back more than 600 years. The split-level interior is a reminder that the building was once separate cottages. Although located just off the High Street it is essentially a community pub equally popular with locals and tourists. It sells **Brakspear Special**, **Nethergate Suffolk County**, **Shepherd Neame Spitfire**, **Fuller's London Pride** and guest beers. Food is available at lunchtimes and

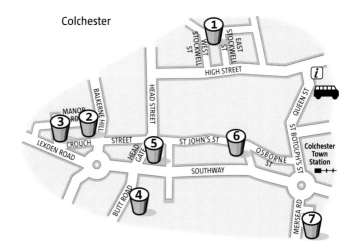

Colchester

Sunday lunches are excellent value for money so booking is advisable (01206 575560). The pub closes during weekend afternoons.

Retrace your steps back up the hill then turn right along the High Street, and left at the junction into Head Street.

It is well worth making a short detour right along Church Street (opposite the Halifax bank) to Colchester Arts Centre, where the annual beer festival is held each May. This historic venue, just inside the Roman wall, was a target during the Civil War as a small, fat cannon sat on top of the tower. During the Siege of Colchester the tower and the cannon, nicknamed Humpty Dumpty, were partially destroyed and the event is remembered in the well-known nursery rhyme.

At the crossroads of Crouch Street and St John's Street turn right into Crouch Street and use the underpass or crossing to get across the busy dual carriageway. On the left, shortly after the crossing, is the **King's Arms** (2). This thriving town-centre pub, that can get busy at times, sells **Adnams Bitter**, **Boddingtons Bitter**, **Flowers Original**, **Greene King Abbot**, **Wadworth 6X** and guest beers which change on a regular basis and there is also a selection of **bottled Belgian beers**. Meals, available at lunchtimes and in the evenings, are reasonably priced and there is authentic Thai food. There is always something going on including live music, quiz nights, and occasional beer festivals. A patio area at the rear provides an ideal spot to enjoy those balmy summer nights.

Continue along Crouch Street to the **Hospital Arms** (3), appropriately situated opposite the hospital. It has now reverted to its previous name following a spell in the 1990s as a Tap and Spile. It is a superb example of a pub that can survive easily without a pool table, fruit machine or juke box. Popular with all ages this is a great pub to meet for a chat and there is a real buzz about the place when it gets busy. The interior initially looks small but further investigation reveals several different drinking areas and a courtyard at the rear. On the hand pulls are **Adnams Bitter**, **Broadside**, **Fisherman** and seasonal beers along with guests. Meals are served at lunchtimes.

Retrace your steps back to the crossroads, this time turning right into Headgate and using the underpass to enter Butt Road by the police station. The **Dragoon** (4) is on the left about 200 yards from the underpass. Although the lounge and public bars in this friendly local have been knocked into one it retains the feel of a two-bar pub. At one end is the quieter lounge area, at the other there is a pool table and large-screen TV where sporting events are regularly shown making it very popular with football fans – it is also the closest decent pub to Colchester United's ground and becomes very busy on match days. Beers include **Adnams Bitter**, **Fisherman** and seasonal choices along with **Everards Tiger** and a guest beer. Lunchtime meals are served, with roast dinners on Sundays, and Friday is fish and chips night.

Retrace your steps to the crossroads, this time turning right into St John's Street. On the right is the **Fox and Fiddler** (5). This free house currently sells **Greene King IPA**, **Old Speckled Hen** and **Crouch Vale Brewers Gold**. The landlord expects to have more beers from local micro-brewers when he has settled in properly.

Go on for half a mile to the **Robin Hood** (6) on the right at the junction with Osborne Street. Beers on hand pump include **Tolly Mild** and **Original** and a guest ale. This is an unusual wedge-shaped pub which at times is loud and lively.

The local Ghost Tour also drops in occasionally so you may be treated to a re-enactment of an unusual incident that happened here in the 1930s.

From the Robin Hood continue along Osborne Street to St Botolph's roundabout by Colchester Town railway station. Use the underpass to exit at the bottom of Mersea Road by the bus stop on the roundabout. Head uphill and after about 300 yards you will find the **Odd One Out** (7) (01206 578140) on the left. This is Colchester's premier real ale free house with a commitment to supporting local breweries. It is basic but comfortable and attracts a wide ranging clientele interested in decent beer and real conversation. In addition to the superb range of up to seven beers including **Archers Best**, **Tolly Original** and guests, there are three ciders and a large range of single malt and Irish whiskies all at extremely competitive prices. Well-behaved dogs and their owners are allowed in the wooden floored bar area and a no-smoking area is sometimes used for meetings.

Retrace your steps to the roundabout and the railway station or continue up St Botolph's Street to return to the bus station.

King's Lynn

UP TO THE 16TH CENTURY this handsome town was Bishop's Lynn and belonged to the See of Norwich. It was then appropriated by Henry VIII at the dissolution of the monasteries. It was not only a flourishing market town but one of England's busiest ports to serve the wool trade and a large fishing fleet. Many fine-looking buildings remain and are passed on this crawl. The 15th-century Guildhall, with its remarkable chequered frontage, contains a sword that may have been given to the town by King John in 1216, just before he lost his royal treasure in a shipwreck in the Wash when fleeing from his rebellious barons.

The first three pubs of the crawl are in the south of the town about 15 minutes' walk from both the railway and bus stations. It starts with the **Stuart House Hotel** (1) at the end of a lane signposted from Goodwins Road. This is a privately-run residential hotel (01553 772169) with a public bar offering a range of three changing ales. It is comfortable and welcoming and a good venue for live jazz and blues. The hotel holds a beer festival in late July which coincides with the King's Lynn Festival. This bar only opens during the evenings and on Sunday lunchtimes.

Move on to the **Live and Let Live** (2) in nearby Windsor Road, a busy locals' bar that has changed little since the middle of last century and has been licensed since 1846. There is an interesting collection of old photographs. The beer menu usually includes a mild, an ordinary strength bitter and a premium bitter, and frequently one of these is from the **Wolf Brewery** in Attleborough. It recently acquired Cask Marque accreditation.

Go across London Road to the next stop, the **London Porterhouse** (3), a small, lively one-roomed bar with barrels behind the bar, a very rare sight these days, with the beer dispensed by gravity. Cooling jackets are used to keep the beer at a correct temperature in all weathers. This is a

King's Lynn

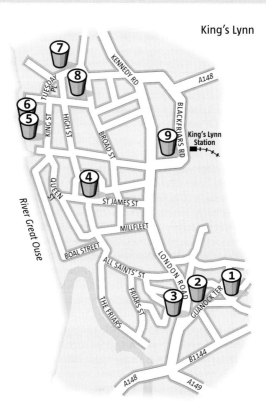

Greene King pub that opens all day serving **IPA** and **Abbot** and a guest beer from its one hand pull. It has been in business since 1864 and has recently been sympathetically refurbished.

Head back to the town centre to the **White Hart Stores** (4) on St James Street, which has been licensed since 1623 and is King's Lynn's oldest continuously licensed premises. It serves three real ales – **Greene King IPA** and two guest beers which may often include a mild.

Go along Queen Street and King Street and turn into Ferry Lane for the **Ouse Amateur Sailing Club** (5). It was CAMRA's national Club of the Year in 1998. This popular club has a one-roomed bar with a verandah overlooking the river. There are up to seven beers and a cider on sale here. **Bateman's** beers are always included on the list and there is usually a strong beer and a dark beer included. Lunch is served every day except Sundays. It closes in the afternoons except on Fridays. Show this guide, the *Good Beer Guide* or a CAMRA membership card for entry.

At the bottom of Ferry Street, off a corner of the Tuesday Market, is the **Crown and Mitre** (6), a one-roomed bar with a nautical theme. The beers here are usually from **Woodforde's** but the licensee has applied for alterations which may include a brewery.

On the other side of the Tuesday Market Place is the **Tudor Rose** (7). This hotel has a front bar and a back bar and is a free house serving three ales. The Tudor Rose is a 15th-century building with oak beams and panelled walls.

Across the car park is the **Lattice House** (8), another 15th-century building with wooden beams. It is owned by Wetherspoon's who have renovated the building while keeping many of its original features. The usual Wetherspoon rules apply – no music, no games, a no-smoking area and a variety of beers.

The finish is at the **Fenman** (9) in Blackfriars Road opposite the railway station. This is a large one-roomed bar decorated with a railway theme and normally selling three beers from **Greene King** – **IPA**, **Abbot** and a guest from the brewery list. It opens all day except Sundays when it closes during the afternoons.

Sheringham and Holt

THIS IS A TWO-TOWN CRAWL linked by a train ride. It starts in Sheringham an attractive seaside resort on the north Norfolk coast and a terminus of the Bittern Line, a main line service that runs from Norwich through Cromer and North Walsham. You can visit three pubs here although there are more if you have the time. Then you take the North Norfolk Railway, a private preserved line, to the pretty little town of Holt where its three pubs are within a stone's throw of one another. If you are lucky your six-mile journey between the two towns may be on a steam train and it might have real ale on sale in the buffet bar. If you are even luckier, instead of walking the final mile from the station into Holt, there's a chance you could travel by an old-fashioned and quite rare horse bus.

However, we start in Sheringham at the main line railway station. Turn right out of here and walk down Station Road and the **Robin Hood Tavern** (1) is on your right. This is an airy, two-roomed pub selling **Greene King Ruddles Best**, **Samuel Smith Old Brewery Bitter** and guest beers. It opens all day and food is served both at lunchtimes and in the evenings. Children are welcome here and there is a family room and a playground in the beer garden.

Take a short walk further down Station Road into where it becomes High Street for the **Lobster** (2) a two-roomed pub where the lounge has been given a fishing theme as befits its nearness to the harbour. **Adnams Bitter**, **Draught Bass**, **Greene King Abbot** and **Marston's Pedigree** and occasionally guest beers from local breweries are on the hand pulls. Food is served at lunchtimes and in the evenings and the pub closes in the afternoons. This is another child-friendly pub with a courtyard and garden.

The next stop is an optional one for it is a good ten minutes' walk from the station. Go back to the station, pass it and turn left into Cromer Road to the *Dunstable Arms* (3)

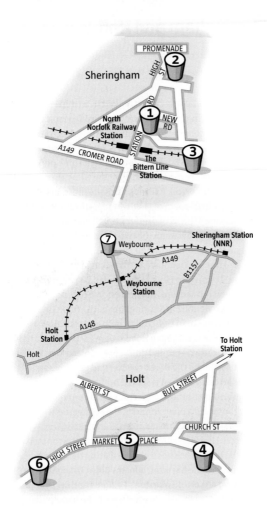

another pub that retains its tap room along with a very comfortable lounge. The prize-winning local brew, **Woodforde's Wherry Best Bitter**, is on sale along with **Courage Directors** and occasional guest beers. The pub is open all day and lunches and dinners are served.

Go back towards your starting point but cross the road to the North Norfolk Line station. Trains to Holt run through the year but the timetable varies to suit the season and the day. It is best to check on 01263 820800. Some services are steam hauled and others are on vintage diesel trains. It's known as the 'Poppy Line' because millions of these flowers grow along the route. At Sheringham there is a visitor centre, a railway museum and a refreshment room. On certain trains – again it's best to ask – there will be real ale on sale in the buffet cars from **Woodforde's Brewery**. The 25-minute journey is just about the right time for a pint.

The journey takes you through the delightful Sheringham Park and over Kelling Heath to Holt Station which is a mile outside of the town. Most trains are met by the 'Holt Flyer' a unique horse bus service that takes you steadily along the mile stretch into Holt passing Gresham's

public school. This delightful market town – Holt is the Saxon word for wood – has an abundance of shops and it is easy to purchase local delicacies such as samphire, herrings, bloaters and crabs.

Your bus stop is in the car park at the **Railway Tavern** (4) which is said to be haunted – stay the night and find out (01263 712259). This old hotel sells **Adnams Bitter**, **Charles Wells Bombardier** and guest beers in summer when it opens all day. The separate restaurant is no-smoking and provides lunches and dinners. There are children's play facilities in the garden.

Walk into the Market Place for the **Feathers** (5) a well-established hotel with overnight accommodation at reasonable rates (01263 712318). It is a **Greene King** house selling **IPA** and **Abbot** and a good selection of wines. There are several rooms including the most popular one which has an open fire, all served from the one bar. Good value bar lunches are served. The bar closes in the afternoons.

A little further along in the High Street is the **King's Head** (6) with its comfortable lounge where lunches are served and there is a public bar. It has a good market town pub atmosphere particularly on Saturdays – a real buzz. There is also an excellent garden. On the hand pumps are **Flowers Original** and **Tolly Original**.

It is an easy walk back to the Railway Tavern for the Flyer but a little longer to the station although there are buses from Holt to Sheringham. However, if your return journey is by train then you might consider stopping off at Weybourne and walking a half mile to the village for the **Ship** (7) an attractive brick and flint building of the early 18th century. It has a comfortable lounge with an open fire, a bar, a dining room and games area. It sells **Greene King IPA** and **Abbot** and guest beers. It closes in the afternoons except on Saturdays. Amongst its many interesting features are the windows from the former Steward and Patteson Brewery.

IT USED TO BE CALLED the West Midlands but no doubt the Heart of England is a more attractive name and it fits the region well with its superb position and all its qualities and attractions. It is a region of marked contrasts and all the more appealing because of this. On the one hand are the Black Country and the Potteries and the great industrial heritage of Birmingham and Coventry and on the other are Shakespeare country, the Forest of Dean, Wenlock Edge, the Lincolnshire coast and delightful market towns of great character.

And the quality of its inns and pubs is unchallenged both in country and in town. You are introduced to eight pub crawls in the Heart of England – three in county towns, two in market towns, another in a village that owns two breweries, one in an inland port and a walk from one county to another through the Malvern Hills. The whole area is easy to access and accommodation is plentiful and geared to suit all pockets. For more information contact the Heart of England Tourist Board on 01905 763436.

Heart of England

Bishop's Castle

BISHOP'S CASTLE is a small border market town in the midst of scenic walking country on the edge of Clun forest. It has three Tudor houses and one of the smallest town halls in England. It is best reached by a regular bus service from Shrewsbury. Only the ancients remember the rail link although the town does boast a tiny transport museum testifying to that part of its history.

Time your visit for the first weekend in July for the annual beer festival in which nearly every pub participates and enjoy street entertainment, barbecues and lots of live music. Most pubs in the town are on the same street and it is really a question of whether you want to drink your way up or down the hill. Be trustful for however much you drink, you cannot get lost.

The crawl begins in Salop Street at the top of the town in the **Three Tuns** (1), which dates from 1642. It serves beers from the John Roberts Brewery such as **XXX** and **Offas** and also offers feistier seasonal brews such as **Old Scrooge**. There is a museum in the adjacent tower brewery. The pub itself is a warren of small bare-boarded rooms with a narrow beer terrace at the rear. Live musical events, particularly jazz, are regular features.

Leave by the front door, turn left and two minutes away, facing you, is the imposing façade of the **Castle Hotel** (2) which commands an excellent

36

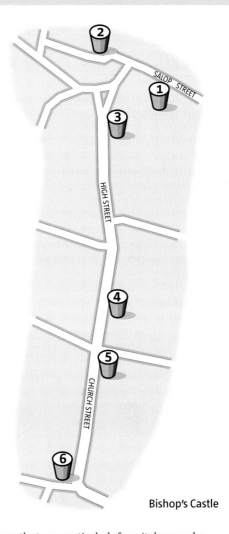

Bishop's Castle

view over the town, particularly from its beer garden.
This is a fine, period hotel with two main public rooms,
a snug and a dining room. It has timeless ambience with
real fires, good food and accommodation (01588 638403).
Six Bells Big Nev's, **Black Sheep Best Bitter**, **Hobsons Best Bitter**

and **Draught Bass** are always available on the hand pumps alongside an excellent range of malt whiskies.

On leaving begin your descent of High Street by passing the ancient town hall on your right and within three minutes you reach the **Crown and Anchor Vaults** (3) on your left. This is two-roomed with sawdust covered wooden floors and dramatic pop art murals, it exudes a laid back Bohemian atmosphere. **Tetley Bitter** and **Salopian Shropshire Gold** are constantly available in the bar.

A short way further down the hill brings you to the *King's Head* (4). **Worthington's Best Bitter** and **Greene King Old Speckled Hen** are the beer options in a two-roomed pub with probably the youngest clientele in the town.

Two minutes walk further and High Street becomes Church Street and on the crossroads is the **Boar's Head** (5) offering beer and bar meals in one long, single room. **Thwaites Bitter**, **Courage Best Bitter** and **Directors** are usually available supplemented by occasional guests often from the local **Salopian Brewery**. Bed and breakfast is also available.

It is a short distance to the final pub, the **Six Bells** (6), a two-roomed 17th-century coaching inn which is situated on an old drovers' road. It offers a friendly welcome and home-cooked food in addition to a range of beers from the small brewery at the rear of the main pub building. Regular brews include **Six Bells Big Nev's** (named after gentle giant, Nev the brewer), **Marathon Ale** and **Cloud Nine**. These are supplemented by stronger seasonal beers and festival specials. The public bar has a basic but comfortable feel and the lounge is carefully furnished and decorated. Brewery tours can be arranged with a bit of advance notice.

It is a short distance back to the bus stop opposite the Boar's Head.

Boston

THE ECONOMY OF this attractive market town today relies on agriculture when once it was one of the busiest ports in England. There is still a limited trade at the dock, particularly fishing, but the harbour these days is partly silted up. Some of the puritans who joined the Pilgrim Fathers were imprisoned here and the Massachusetts city of Boston where they landed took its name from here. It is said to be 'Botolph's Town' and the parish church is St Botolph's, better known as the 'Boston Stump' and so-called because it has no spire. Nevertheless it is the second highest church in Lincolnshire and can be seen for miles across the fens.

The pub scene is interesting with many old pubs that are comparatively unspoilt and there is a decent range of beers, some good food and plenty of accommodation.

Start at the railway station by turning right down Station Approach and turning left into Queen Street and immediately left into West Street for the **Eagle** (1) a Tynemill house that has recently been refurbished. The small lounge is comfortable and made doubly so in winter by a coal fire. It sells **Adnams Broadside**, **Banks's Bitter**, **Taylor Landlord** and an ever-changing selection of guest beers and the food is good value. It closes during the afternoons from Mondays to Thursdays.

Walk back to Queen Street and follow this to the roundabout and then take John Adams Way and after half a mile go left into Main Ridge, right into Silver Street and the **Coach and Horses** (2), a locals' pub that offers a very warm welcome. There is just the one cosy and comfortable bar selling **Bateman XB** and **XXXB**. There is a great community spirit with sports teams abounding and it is very popular with supporters of Boston United whose ground is quite near.

Carry on Silver Street turning right into Wide Bargate for the **New England Hotel** (3). This residential hotel (01205 365255) was built as an inn in 1830 on the site of a former one.

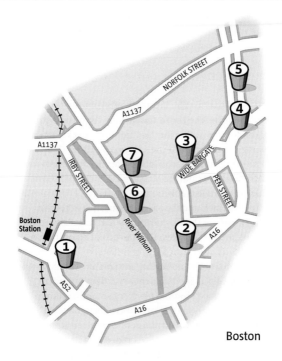

Boston

The car park was once the poultry market. The Imperial bar and the foyer have some beautiful decorative plaster ceilings. The beer range varies with guest ales constantly changing and a wide range of British and foreign bottled beers, more than 80 vodkas and 30 whiskies, make this an interesting place to visit. And the food in both the bar and the restaurant is highly recommended. It is a very comfortable place and it opens all day.

Cross the road into Pen Street and turn right into Horncastle Road and continue until you reach the **Cowbridge** (4) just to the north of the town centre. It has three main areas, a no-nonsense public bar decorated with scarves of football clubs, a comfy lounge with an open fire and a restaurant serving excellent freshly-prepared food at lunchtimes and early evenings. **Theakston Mild** is a permanent fixture on the bars supplemented by a constantly-changing selection of guest beers. The pub closes in the afternoons.

Stay on Horncastle Road for a short distance to the **Roper's Arms** (5), a quiet corner pub owned by local Lincolnshire brewer **Bateman** with beers from its portfolio and always including **XB**. There is occasional live entertainment. It opens from 2 pm but this extends to all day at weekends and in the summer. Nearby is the Maud Foster Mill, one of the few working windmills in the country, built in 1819. It is unusual in having five sails rather than the usual four.

Carry on Horncastle Road and turn left at Norfolk Street and continue until you reach Witham Place – turn left for 120 yards then bear left into Wormgate for **Goodbarns Yard** (6) which has a wonderful position by the river and a great view of the Boston Stump. There are beams in the original buildings, possibly artisans' cottages, comfortable settles in assorted alcoves, a new extension with a riverside terrace and a generally old-fashioned and comfortable atmosphere. It sells **Courage Directors**, **Greene King Old Speckled Hen**, **Theakston XB** and guest beers and has a good reputation for its food. It opens all day.

Retrace your steps to Witham Place and after 50 yards turn right again for Witham Street and the **Carpenter's Arms** (7) a pleasant, street-corner, long-established local with bare floorboards selling **Draught Bass**, **Batemans XB** and occasionally its **Mild** along with guest beers. Good lunches and filled rolls are served. Bed and breakfast is available (01205 362840).

Go back to the end of Witham Place, turn left and follow the road round crossing the River Witham and turning left into Irby Street which leads into Irby Place. Then turn right on to Tower Street and right again for Station Street which leads to Station Approach and your finishing point.

Leominster

THIS DELIGHTFUL MARKET TOWN is set amongst cider apple orchards, hop fields and sheep and cattle grazing country – Herefordshire cattle are exported from here all over the world. Leominster has a most amazing collection of architectural styles: Tudor, Jacobean and Georgian through to modern day – and the parish church, formerly a priory, and the relocated 17th-century town hall are both worth visiting. There is also a folk museum with a strong agricultural influence.

From the train station turn right towards the town centre into Etnam Street. The **Chequers** (1) is on the right. This superb black white timber-framed structure has a lively public bar at the front and a quieter lounge and dining area at the rear. It is the oldest pub in the town, built in 1480. **Banks's** beers are served with guests from the **Dunn Plowman** range. It opens all day and food is available at lunchtimes and in the evenings.

Next, a few doors along, you come to the **Bell** (2), which serves **Draught Bass** and one beer from the **Dunn Plowman Brewery**. This is an open-plan pub with a U-shaped bar. There is live music on Thursday evenings.

Turn left into South Street to the **Black Horse** (3) on the right. This former coaching inn was the home of the **Dunn Plowman Brewery** in the early 1990s. At that time it was based in an outbuilding, and was thought to be the smallest brewery in Britain. However, increased demand for the beers led them to seek larger premises. The beers are still sold along with **Hobsons Town Crier** and guest ales. Bar snacks and meals are served, but not on Sundays. It has a public bar, a narrow lounge and a dining area to the rear. Pétanque and quoits are played here.

Retrace your steps back along South Street to the town centre, and come to two residential hotels: the *Royal Oak* (4), (01586 612610) which may have a traditional beer on sale,

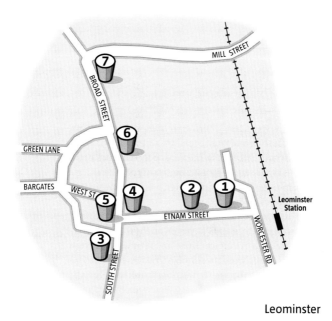

Leominster

and the *Talbot Hotel* (5) (01586 616347) which sells just one –
Greene King Ruddles Best. Both have good standard
accommodation.

Continue north into Broad Street, to the **Grapes Vaults**
(6). Beers are from the **Marston's** and **Banks's** ranges along
with a guest and there is a wide range of simple, freshly-
cooked food. This is a well preserved two-roomed pub,
welcoming and attractive, with etched windows, original
dark high-backed settles, coal fires, a bottle collection, old
local prints and posters, and no machines or canned music.

Head north towards the outskirts of the town as far as
the **Hop Pole** (7). The beer range here includes **Marston's**
Pedigree and a beer from the former **SP Sporting Ales** range
now brewed by **Dunn Plowman**. Food is served from freshly-
prepared ingredients and the portions are generous.
It is but a short, gentle walk back to the railway station.

Through the Malvern Hills

In a somer seson whan soft was the sonne.
WILLIAM LANGLAND *Piers Plowman*

THE MALVERN HILLS form part of the border between Herefordshire and Worcestershire and the area is very popular with hikers. The medieval poet William Langland used it as the setting for his allegorical poem *Piers Plowman* and, five centuries later, it was the inspiration of the composer Edward Elgar.

This crawl starts at Colwall train station, on the line between Hereford and Worcester, on the west side of the Malvern Hills in Herefordshire, and finishes at Malvern Link Station in Worcestershire. Whilst it is possible to do the crawl in the opposite direction Malvern Link enjoys more frequent train services to Worcester, Birmingham and London. The walk is about five miles and visits six widely differing pubs.

Leave Colwall Station and immediately on the right is the **Colwall Park Hotel** (1). This sells two real ales, one from the **Highgate** range and one from one of the local micros. It also serves a range of food, all prepared from fresh local ingredients. It is residential (01684 540206). The nearby *Crown Inn* sells one or two mainstream ales.

Turn right and pass the Schweppes works, where Malvern water is bottled, then follow Walwyn Road (B4218) up the hill and after about 20 minutes you come to a hairpin bend. Take the minor road that goes off to the right and after 200 yards you arrive at the **Chase Inn** (2). This two-bar pub is one of the few outlets for **Donnington** beers west of the River Severn with **SBA** on the taps. In addition there is **Hobsons Best Bitter** and two beers from the **Wye Valley Brewery**: **HPA**, and one of the **Dorothy Goodbody** seasonal ales. Food is available here at lunchtimes. In summer the garden at the rear enjoys excellent views across

44

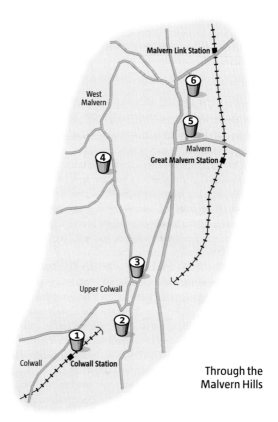

Malvern Link Station

West
Malvern

Malvern
Great Malvern Station

Upper Colwall

Colwall   Colwall Station

Through the
Malvern Hills

Herefordshire to the Welsh Mountains including the
Brecon Beacons.

Retrace your steps to the hairpin bend and turn right up
the hill until you come to a cutting at the top. The road
bends round to the left here and on the right there is a
sheer drop as the hillside falls away and, on most days,
there is an excellent view of the Severn Valley. On the left is
the **Wyche Inn** (3) a large two-roomed pub with several pool
tables and electronic games. The beer range includes beers
from the **Malvern Hills** and the **St George's** breweries. Food is
served all afternoon at weekends and is reasonably priced.

Go back towards the cutting and a steep path leads to the crest of the hill where it soon joins with the metalled path that leads up to the top of the Worcester Beacon, highest peak of the Malvern Hills at 1395ft. However, you will turn off at a 'directional fruitcake', a circular direction indicator made out of Malvern granite. Take the path to the left taking you down to a quarry that in 1968 was used by the BBC to film a *Doctor Who* story starring Patrick Troughton. From here you drop down to the West Malvern road (B4232) which you follow for about half a mile until a sign on the left reads 'Brewers Arms 70 yards'.

Follow as indicated down an unmade track to the **Brewers Arms** (4). This gem of a pub was badly damaged a few years ago, but following representations by the locals to the owners, Marston's, it was rebuilt very sympathetically. The beers are from **Marston's** and food is available at both lunchtimes and in the evenings up to 9 pm. Live folk music sessions take place on Tuesday nights.

Head back up the track, cross over the road and climb a steeply graded track called the Dingle. This brings you to the crest of the hill to the north of the Worcester Beacon. Here is another 'directional fruitcake' and from it take the path down the hill signed for Malvern town centre and St Ann's well. The latter is a café in a remarkable octagonal structure built in Victorian times. Although not licensed, it is an excellent place to stop for a cup of tea.

The track zigzags down and brings us to the top of the 99 steps. At the bottom of these is the *Mount Pleasant Hotel*, and 100 yards further along is the *Unicorn*, Malvern's oldest pub. Go down Church Street and turn left at the traffic lights for the **Great Malvern Hotel** (5) a Victorian hotel in the bustling town centre. This is a good place to stay if visiting Malvern to enjoy a play or concert at the nearby Winter Gardens (01684 563411). The beer range includes **Hobsons Best Bitter**, **Wood Shropshire Lad**, **Fuller's London Pride** and guest beers. Good food is served taking full advantage of local produce.

On leaving turn left and head along the road for about half a mile, turn left again up Moorlands Road until you come to the **Nag's Head** (6). This is a large open-plan pub

Great
Malvern
Hotel

with pool table and other games and it has a wide range of beers including a **Malvern Hills** beer and **Wood Shropshire Lad** together with several guest beers. Live music is often held in the annexe, called the Nag's Tail.

From here it is a short, attractive walk across the common to Malvern Link train station. And on the way home you may reflect on Piers Plowman's thoughts which are roughly translated from medieval English:

And on a May morning on Malvern hills
I fell asleep for weariness of wandering.

Newark-on-Trent

KING JOHN DIED HERE – from over-eating no less and maybe incorporating a few drinks too many. And whatever the inn and tavern scene was like in 1216 it is certainly excellent almost eight centuries later. Newark-upon-Trent, to give it its full name, is a fine town in many ways set off by one of the most impressive market places in England – cobbled and surrounded by Georgian buildings and some fine pubs, one of which we visit on this crawl and in another one Byron lodged while publishing his first book of poems. It has great history too: Lady Godiva owned it in the 11th century, John fought and defeated the barons here before his gluttonous death and Gladstone made his first political speech here from a window in the square. The crawl starts from the bus station.

Walk down Lombard Street and turn right into Castle Gate and right again into Stodman Street where the **Woolpack** (1) is on your right. This is a cosy, multi-roomed, unspoilt pub with a bar, lounge and smoke room, a patio and a long alley skittles pitch. It is said to be the oldest trading pub in Newark and was built in 1465. **John Smith's Bitter** and guest beers are sold. Good value food is served at lunchtimes and in the early evenings, with breakfasts from 9am. It closes during the afternoons. Bed and breakfast is available (01636 704326).

Continue up Stodman Street into Bridge Street for the **Wing Tavern** (2), hidden away in the corner of the Market Square. This unspoilt spit 'n' sawdust pub is a gem. It has a bar, pool room, small family room, patio and is another long alley skittles venue. **Theakston Bitter**, **XB** and **Old Peculier** are on the hand pulls. It closes in the afternoons.

Across Appletongate is the **Fox and Crown** (3) that belongs to the Tynemill group which had its birth pangs in Newark. The pub is open-plan but with comfortable nooks and corners, including no-smoking family areas. There are

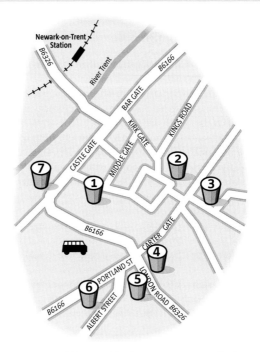

stone and wood floors and big brewery mirrors and other breweriana on display. **Castle Rock Nottingham Gold** (Tynemill owns the brewery), **Everards Tiger**, **Hook Norton Best Bitter**, **Caledonian Deuchars IPA** and guest ales are sold together with farm cider and perry, dozens of malt whiskies, continental draught and bottled beers, flavoured vodkas and a good choice of wines. There is good value food with an emphasis on local produce, served at lunchtimes and in the evenings. It opens all day.

Turn back into Carter Gate as far as London Road and on the nearside corner is a former coaching inn, the **Mail Coach** (4). This busy one-roomed pub has three distinct areas inside and a patio. There is live music on Thursdays. On the hand pumps are **Boddingtons Bitter**, **Flowers IPA** and **Original** and guest beers. There is food at lunchtimes. It closes in the afternoons except on Saturdays when it remains open all day. And there is accommodation (01636 605164).

Across London Road – almost opposite – is the **Castle and Falcon** (5), a traditional two-roomed pub with a function room and a family area. It is popular with young and old and is big on lots of sports with more than 20 teams located here. **John Smith's Bitter** and guest ales which change regularly are sold and tasters are offered. The pub opens every evening and at lunchtimes except on Tuesdays and Thursdays.

Turn left out of the pub then left again into Portland Street and, on the left is the **Horse and Gears** (6). This is a small friendly local that is popular with darts players but most welcoming to visitors. It sells **Mansfield Cask Ale** and **Marston's Pedigree**.

A final call could be made by walking down Pelham Street and turning right into Mill Gate and spending some time at the excellent Mill Gate Museum of Social and Folk Life. However, if it's a final pub call you want then walk on to where Castle Gate starts and there, in Swan and Salmon Yard, is **Kelly's Tavern** (7). This is an appropriate name for what is presently the only mainland tied house of **Okells Brewery** from the Isle of Man. It also sells guest beers from local micros. There is an ornate high-ceilinged bar with attractive windows, lots of old Manx pictures and pleasant alcoves with river and lock views. The quiet upstairs room has a balcony and there is a terrace and garden. Bar food is served by friendly staff and it opens all day.

Shrewsbury

THE HANDSOME COUNTY TOWN of Shropshire stands on a horseshoe bend of the River Severn where ten bridges cross it. It dates from Roman times and has great history. In the fifth and sixth centuries it was the seat of the Welsh princes of Powys and later became part of the Kingdom of Mercia. Shrewsbury Castle was built in 1083 and rebuilt by Edward I in the 13th century and is now the home of the Shropshire Regimental Museum. It was a strategic stronghold on the Welsh border.

The 11th-century abbey survived the dissolution of the monasteries and remains a parish church to this day. Shrewsbury public school was founded in 1552 by Edward VI and Sir Philip Sidney and Charles Darwin were scholars there. During the English Civil War both Charles I and his nephew Prince Rupert established their headquarters there for short periods. The town claims 660 listed buildings, many of them half-timbered. The medieval street pattern remains including the 'shuts' and passages that weave their way through the town centre.

There are around 90 pubs in Shrewsbury, of which about 30 are within the river loop – and your tour will take in five of these with one outside the loop. The best way to arrive is by train – not too difficult a task when one considers that there are five different lines radiating out from Shrewsbury. The bus station in Raven Meadows is about 200 yards along the route of the crawl.

Before leaving the station, which is on one of the ten bridges, turn around on the forecourt to look up at the castle and back at the station which celebrated its 150th anniversary in 1998. The station started with only two floors, surprisingly the top two, with the ground floor added later!

The crawl is anticlockwise and so saves the best to the last. Walk along Smithfield Road, crossing over if you want

51

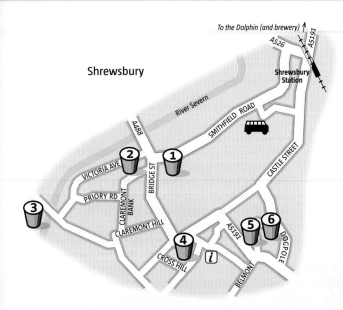

good views of the river. Pass the bus station then, just before the Welsh Bridge, on the left is the **Shrewsbury Hotel** (1), a Wetherspoon pub with nine beers at the last count including **Greene King Abbot**, **Hop Back Summer Lightning**, **Shepherd Neame Spitfire** and **Theakston Best Bitter**. The large L-shaped room has a smoke-free dining area. There is no canned music and the pub is open all day. Accommodation is available (01743 340382).

After the first brisk stroll just go round the corner to the **Armoury** (2) in Victoria Avenue, a large upmarket free house that fronts the quayside in the middle of Shrewsbury's newest entertainment area. It was converted from an armoury in 1995. It has interesting decor and excellent food complementing five constantly-changing guest beers. Regular beers on the hand pulls are **Boddingtons Bitter**, **Wadworth 6X** and **Wood Shropshire Lad** and also on sale are more than 70 malt whiskies and 20 bourbons.

On leaving turn left, keeping the river on your right, and go into Quarry Park to the Port Hill Footbridge.

Cross over to reach the **Boathouse** (3) which is owned by
Wharfedale Taverns and takes its six or seven cask beers
from Carlsberg-Tetley Tapsters' Choice range of mainly
regional independent breweries. It has an imposing
position on the River Severn. There are three rooms
with bare boards, oak pillars and dark wood panelling with
advertising posters from long-gone Shrewsbury
businesses. The cellars have a grisly secret, having been
used as a charnel house for victims of the plague.

From here retrace your steps over the footbridge but
this time go up the sloping park path towards the domed
tower of St Chad's Church dominating the skyline.
By looking behind you and across the river to your right you
will see another skyline dominated this time by some of

the buildings of the famous Shrewsbury
public school. On leaving the park, cross
the road and take the first left, then go
down to Cross Street and along it to the
Coach and Horses (4) on the corner of
Swan Hill. This is a busy, thriving
town-centre pub in the Victorian style.
It has a wood-panelled bar and a larger
restaurant to the rear where the food is
first class and reasonably priced. Real ales
on sale are **Draught Bass** and up to five
guests, with **Shropshire Gold** from the
Salopian Brewery a popular choice.
The pub opens all day.

After the Coach and Horses, turn left
and at the bottom turn right and then
go diagonally across the square and up
Grope Lane, one of the many 'shuts'
of Shrewsbury, and right at the end in
Fish Street is the **Three Fishes** (5), one of
the first completely smoking free pubs
in the country. The pub fits well into the
most attractive street in the shadow of
two churches. The original four rooms
have been knocked out but much of the
timbers and stone flagging remain and

53

retain its character. **Adnams Bitter**, **Fuller's London Pride**, **Taylor Landlord** and guest beers are on the bar and food is served except on Sunday evenings. It was the local CAMRA Pub of the Year in 2002.

Retrace your steps back up Fish Street and up through Bear Steps into St Alkmund's Square and across it into Church Street for the classic pub of this crawl, the **Loggerheads** (6), a Grade II listed building with its original four-roomed layout retained. It has been described as 'unspoilt by progress'. Two bars are served from a hatchway in a stone-flagged corridor. Another bar, formerly 'gentlemen only', has settles and scrubbed tables and the fourth is tiny and wood-panelled. It is tied to Wolverhampton & Dudley Breweries and sells **Banks's Original** and **Bitter**, **Marston's Pedigree**, **Draught Bass** and guest ales which change regularly. Food is available except on Sundays which is the only day the pub closes in the afternoons, reopening at 8pm. There is a no music policy.

After the Loggerheads turn right and make your way back to the railway station. Buses go from the bus station to Bishop's Castle where there is another crawl in this book. If you are staying the night or have time on your hands, then a ten-minute amble to the *Good Beer Guide* listed *Dolphin* in St Michael's Street to the north of the station, is worth while. It is the home of the Dolphin Brewery, is gaslit and has late opening.

Stafford

THIS IS A BUSTLING COUNTY TOWN with loads of history and plenty to see. The town was mentioned in the Domesday Book and it suffered in the Civil War when its castle and town walls were destroyed. The Georgian Shire Hall in the Market Place is now an art gallery and the four-storeyed High House in Mill Street claims to be the largest timber-framed house in England. Izzak Walton the author of *The Complete Angler* was born here and there is a bust of him in the parish church and Richard Brinsley Sheridan, who was the town's MP for 16 years, lived in what is now the post office. For those who arrive by train the Stafford Arms is a welcoming sight. In this crawl we will maintain a tradition of starting elsewhere and leaving the best until last.

From the station walk right along Station Road, turning left into Newport Road then taking the left turn into Bridge Street – the main shopping street – and on the left and difficult to miss is the **Picture House** (1). This is a very large Wetherspoon pub in a converted cinema that is really well done. It is a Grade II listed building. There are three floor levels with the entrance area reserved for non-smokers.

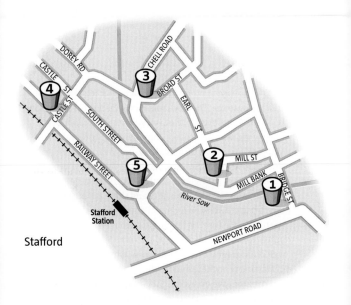

Stafford

A cinema screen has been retained behind the bar. It sells **Banks's Original, Boddingtons Bitter, Courage Directors, Greene King Abbot, Shepherd Neame Spitfire**, guest beers and **Lichfield cider**. The pub is open all day and food is served well into the evenings. Despite its size it can get crowded at weekends. The pub is next to the river and has an extensive terrace.

Go left along Bridge Street and turn into Mill Street (not Mill Bank) and on the right is the **Bird-in-Hand** (2), a four-roomed town-centre pub built in the 1920s by the now closed, local Joules Brewery. There is a quiet snug, a large, comfortable lounge, a games room and a public bar. It is popular with students but attracts a very catholic range of customers. It sells **Courage Best Bitter** and **Directors**, **John Smith's Bitter** and **Worthington's Bitter**. It opens all day and lunches are served.

Turn right and right into Earl Street and at the top in Broad Eye (the Inner Ring Road) is the **Lamb** (3) a former street-corner local which has been extensively refurbished by Punch Taverns that acquired it in 1999. It serves **Banks's Original**, **Draught Bass**, **Everards Tiger** and occasional guest beers through the hand pumps. It is a bright, airy, welcoming hostelry, offering good value food. The pub is opposite Stafford's famous windmill. It serves lunches all week but evening meals up to 8 pm from Mondays to Thursdays only.

Cross the ring road and continue along Broad Eye until you reach Castle Street. Go along here and the **Railway** (4) is on the right. The inn and the surrounding terraced housing date from about 1837 when the Grand Junction railway reached Stafford. It is the best example in the town of a Victorian street-corner local and what changes have been made have been done sensitively. It sells **Draught Bass**, **Greene King Abbot**, **Tetley Bitter** and a guest ale. It only opens in the evenings except at weekends when there are lunchtime sessions.

Continue along Castle Street and turn into Railway Street for the short walk to the **Stafford Arms** (5) opposite the station. This was formerly a Titanic tied house and although it is now owned by Punch Taverns the beer link remains. **Titanic Best Bitter** and **White Star** and several guest beers are on sale and one of the guests can often be from **Titanic** with others from mainly small independent breweries. It has by far the best range of beers in Stafford and also sells traditional cider. The pub has accommodation (01785 253313) and serves good value meals both at lunchtimes and in the evenings during the week and it also does Sunday lunches. It opens all day except on Sunday afternoons. It was Stafford and Stone branch of CAMRA's Pub of the Decade for the 1990s.

Worcester

WORCESTER earned its title of *Civitas fidelis* (the Faithful city) due to its loyalty to the Royalist cause during the English Civil War. This loyalty was mainly due to a Royalist garrison being present in the city, though evidence has shown that the citizens were in fact extremely indifferent, and frequently hostile, to both factions. And in the Battle of Worcester in 1651, Cromwell finally defeated the army of Charles II. The city can lay claim to being one of the longest continually inhabited settlements in Britain, with evidence showing that people have lived here continuously since at least the fifth century AD. The city has been an important market town, particularly for hops, corn and malt and the making of porcelain still continues at the Royal Worcester porcelain works that was founded in 1788.

This pub crawl, which takes in quite a bit of Worcester's history, can start at either the Foregate railway station, or the bus station, both of which are centrally located. If arriving by train, on leaving the station turn left along Foregate Street, take the next left down Sansome Street. From the bus station go into Angel Place, turn left and then right into Shaw Street. Cross over Foregate Street into Sansome Street passing the old Hop Market Commercial Hotel built in 1900 and a reminder of the trade's former importance.

At the junction with Sansome Walk cross over into Lowesmoor and towards the end on the right is the **Apple Tree** (1), a traditional three-storey Georgian cider house – the only one in Worcester – with a snug and balcony area. It sells several ciders, some of which are home brewed, and a single cask ale from the local **St George's Brewery**. The walls are decorated with limited edition comics and fantasy artwork. There is a great table football game in the main bar area and live music on Fridays and Saturdays. It opens all day, every day.

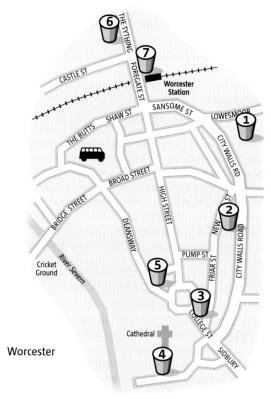

Worcester

Walk back along Lowesmoor and use the pedestrian crossing into Queen Street. Go past the car park into New Street. On the left is the King Charles House originally built by the wealthy brewer Richard Durrant. It is reputed that Charles II fled from the rear of this building after the defeat of his forces in 1651. A few doors down is the **Swan with Two Nicks** (2) a vibrant, multi-level free house with extensive oak fittings and beams and a large collection of enamel signs. Watch your head as you explore its various nooks and crannies. On the hand pulls are **Boddingtons Bitter** and three ever-changing guest beers usually including one from a local micro. It also stocks a huge selection of single malt whiskies. Lunches are served in the upstairs restaurant or the bar. A chess club meets on Tuesday evenings and bridge is played every Sunday. This pub is open through the day but only in the evenings on Sundays.

Turn left and walk along New Street into Friar Street, where you will see several late 16th and early 17th-century houses. Towards the bottom on the left-hand side you will pass the Cardinals Hat, Worcester's oldest public house but presently closed. At the junction of Friar Street and College Street is the Cask Marque accredited **Ye Olde Talbot Hotel** (3). This former coaching inn dates back to the 13th century and today offers 28 en-suite bedrooms, (01905 23573) a 40-seater restaurant and a public bar offering **Greene King Abbot**, **IPA** and **Old Speckled Hen**, as well as two guest beers, which you can drink in front of a real fire in the winter months.

Turn left and pass the Warner Village cinema, then cross over College Street at the pedestrian crossing. Walk up Edgar Street, noting the 14th-century Edgar Tower in front of you. This was built by King John as a gatehouse to the castle that used to stand here. It is now the main entrance to the cathedral precincts. Follow the road around to the left and enter Severn Street. On the left is the main entrance to the Royal Worcester Porcelain factory and immediately on your right is the **Salmon's Leap** (4). It is built on the site of the Fountain Inn which was demolished about 1950. Inside is a collection of pump clips of the many cask beers sold since the landlord took over the pub. **Taylor Landlord** is a regularly available beer along with four ever-changing guest beers from around the country. Meals are available at lunchtimes and in the evenings. On fine Saturday summer evenings there are barbecues in the beer garden.

Return past the Edgar Tower and walk up the steps into College Precinct. Worcester Cathedral is on your left – check your £20 notes for another view. There was a cathedral on this site as early as AD 680 and the current one is based on the plan of Bishop Wulstan's grand Romanesque structure built between 1089 and 1094 but the tower was not completed until 1374. Amongst those buried inside are wicked King John, whose treachery towards his brother Richard left the country in turmoil at his death. His tomb, in the choir, was opened in 1797 and shreds of a monk's cowl were found over his head, giving credence to the story that he had asked to be buried disguised as a monk to improve his chances of getting into heaven. Henry VIII's elder brother, Prince Arthur, was also buried here after his death whilst on honeymoon with Catherine of Aragon.

Walk past the front of the cathedral and follow the road into Deansway. At the second pedestrian crossing go over the road to the **Plough** (5) a listed two-roomed pub serving **Shepherd Neame Spitfire** along with two, often local, guest beers. Light snacks are available at lunchtimes. There are hidden priest holes and rumoured smuggling tunnels to the River Severn from the cellar, rumoured because nobody dare go down them. The landlord is proud of his Basque origins and his nickname of 'Tony Never Opens' – is the result of the slightly idiosyncratic opening hours which include closing in the afternoons, all day Mondays and Sunday lunchtimes – got that? And make sure your mobile phone is turned off as any calls – in or out – will result in a fine with the money going to charity.

From here go down Fish Street to the main shopping precinct, then turn left into High Street which becomes Foregate Street, passing the recently restored Guildhall dating from 1724, and the Greek revival Shire Hall, which opened in 1835. The statue of Queen Victoria is missing one important feature – a wedding ring. Also spot the Postal Order on your right – you will be returning this way.

Enter The Tything and on the left is the **Dragon Inn** (6) for the largest choice of regularly-changing cask beers in Worcester. On the bar will be a selection of seven cask ales, some of which have been personally collected from all over the country by the owners in their little red van. Included will be a mild and, in the winter, stouts and porters. Lunchtime meals and snacks are available and can be eaten alfresco in the summer. This Grade II listed Georgian ale house has recently been refurbished. It closes in the afternoons but is open all day on Saturdays.

Retrace your route to the **Postal Order** (7), which occupies the former telephone exchange but gets its name from a post office that originally occupied the site. As you would expect for a Wetherspoon pub this is a large venue with low price beers and food. There are several regular beers including **Theakston Best Bitter**, **Shepherd Neame Spitfire**, **Greene King Abbot** and **Courage Directors**, along with two or three guest beers. It is Cask Marque accredited. The pub offers a quiet, music and smoke-free end to this pub crawl, unless it is on Friday or Saturday evenings when the crowd at the bar is several deep and even the noise of conversation can be distracting.

It is but a few yards back to the railway station and a little bit further for buses.

London by Pub

EVERYBODY HAS A LONDON. For some, like us up 't'north, it is practically everywhere within a radius of 20 miles of Trafalgar Square, or perhaps the entirety of the underground railway system, even the whole of the world south of Watford. For some purists it is 'within the sound of Bow bells' and for others, like myself who lived there for long enough to know and enjoy it, it is the area of the former, dear departed London County Council. And for other folk it is the London postal districts or Ken Livingstone's fiefdom or The City, that tiny anachronistic enclave, the square mile, that maintains a Lord Mayor and its own police force. For Ted Bruning it is wherever he can find good pubs – mainly within the Circle Line with brief visits south of the river to Greenwich and Southwark and a trip to rural Hampstead. It is all in his book *London by Pub*. He has been kind enough to allow me to plunder it to select, shorten and edit three crawls: Hampstead, Kensington and The City.

Ted Bruning is clear as to what you can expect in London:

There's one special delight that walkers in London can enjoy and walkers in the country can't: pubs. Not that the country has no pubs, although it has fewer every year. And not that there's anything wrong with country pubs – the best of them are the best in the world. But in the country, they're so far apart you can die of thirst as you toil from one to another. In London, they're everywhere. At the slightest excuse – a minor inclemency in the weather, an incipient call of nature, the earliest apprehension of impending thirst – you can dive into the nearest pub, where you will find the answer to whatever ails you. Not that you need an excuse, of course; a whim will do perfectly well.

London pubs of real antiquity are few and far between. There are a handful of 16th and 17th-century survivals, and a larger smattering of 18th-century pubs in enclaves such as Hampstead. But just as most of London is late Georgian and Victorian, so are most of its finest pubs. It does not follow, however, that there is any lack of variety. You will encounter tiny mews pubs, built in the narrow streets and yards behind the mansions of the nobility, and catering for the huge population of servants who ran the aristocratic households. You will visit huge, garish gin-palaces, competing brashly with their neighbours in the capital's main thoroughfares. You will be invited into the hidden haunts of off-duty City types, tucked away in the maze of courts and alleys that in many cases still follow the medieval street-plan. In an afternoon you can move between centuries, between worlds.

And these pubs are not only worthy of a visit for themselves, for their architecture, for their history, for their atmosphere: they are also a key to recreating London as it was. So much of London has changed beyond recognition even in the last 20 years that it seems sometimes to have no history. Only its pubs survive, like Hansel's pebbles, to mark out a way through the wilderness.

There are no maps for these three crawls because the many streets within each area would make it difficult to reproduce them to manageable sizes. The Geographers *A–Z London Street Atlas* is highly recommended and conveniently sized and the London Underground map is invaluable. There is, however, a map for the trip in Wandsworth around Britain's oldest brewery.

The City: After the Fire

Oh, London is a fine town,
  A very famous city,
Where all the streets are paved with gold,
  And all the maidens pretty. George Colman

THE CONSEQUENCES OF THE FIRE that broke out in a baker's shop in Pudding Lane in the early hours of Sunday the second of September 1666 are such that today when we walk through what we call 'the city' we have the bizarre experience of passing between gleaming new towers of the 21st century whose ground-plan was determined by the allocation of building plots in the 11th. You will see little that is truly old; yet away from the Victorian thoroughfares, which were blasted through the old pre-fire street-plan, you will be pacing lines laid out for you 1,000 years ago. And a word of caution before setting out on this particular crawl: pubs in the city often close either part or all of the weekend. It's an old tradition dating from when everywhere shut down on Friday nights. Now, sadly, it's only the pubs.

We start at Blackfriars Station on the District and Circle lines. Cross Queen Victoria Street and the **Blackfriar** (1) is immediately opposite the station. It opens all day during the week and Saturday lunchtimes but closes on Sundays. It sells **Adnams Bitter**, **Fuller's London Pride** and **Draught Bass** and serves bar food at lunchtimes.

Turn left out of the pub into Queen Victoria Street, go immediately left up Blackfriars Lane, and right into Playhouse Yard. Continue along Ireland Yard where Shakespeare bought a house in 1613 for £140; this is his only known London address. In St Andrew's Hill is the **Cockpit** (2) which, although it claims a date of 1787, actually dates from the 1830s and had its own cockpit until the sport was outlawed in 1846.

Its present character, however, dates to a complete remodelling of the 1890s, when it was turned into an Olde English extravaganza. The modest exterior with its theatrical black and gold fascia, leaded-light windows, and big carriage lamps, does not hint at the mock-Tudor kitsch of the interior, which despite recent alterations still includes a minstrels' gallery. It's not exactly a full-sized gallery; in fact you'd have to be a minstrel of restricted growth to be able to use it. On the hand pumps are: **Courage Best Bitter** and **Directors** and **Marston's Pedigree**. It opens 11 am to 11 pm from Mondays to Fridays, closes at 9 pm on Saturdays and during the afternoons on Sundays. Food is served at lunchtimes and early evenings during the week.

Turn left out of the pub and right into Carter Lane and, emerging from its narrows, you are suddenly treated to a vision of the south side of St Paul's, and the scale not only of Wren's masterpiece but also of his entire artistic vision is dramatically revealed. Skirt St Paul's to the south and enjoy another vista of the cathedral, which has been opened up with the construction of the Millennium footbridge. Ignore, however, the big pub called the Centre Page and continue down Cannon Street. Turn left into Bow Lane, cross Watling Street, and turn immediately left into Grovelands Court for **Williamson's Tavern** (3). This was the site of the new Lord Mayor's house after the Great Fire; the wrought iron gates, originally at the mouth of the court, were donated by William and Mary and include their initials. The house was not considered grand enough, however, and in 1739 it was sold to one Robert Williamson to convert into a hotel. Williamson's, despite its past, was never an especially grand hotel and generations of poor maintenance meant that the whole place had to be pulled down in the 1930s. Its replacement is a fine and extremely popular example of '30s design: its two ground-floor bars are spacious, airy and elegant, with a fine plaster ceiling and a Jacobean-style fireplace incorporating supposedly Roman tiles in the front bar. Real ales on the bar include **Brakspear Bitter**, **Greene King IPA**, **Adnams Bitter**, **Fuller's London Pride** and **Draught Bass**. It opens all day from Mondays to Fridays and serves food at lunchtimes and early evening but closes at weekends.

Return to Watling Street for the **Olde Watling** (4). This pub always claims to have been built in 1668 to house the workers who built St Paul's – a claim shared with the

Old Bell in Fleet Street on the other side of the cathedral. We do know it was restored in 1901.

It's all very stern and mannish. There are oak posts and beams, supposedly old ship's timbers – which may be true, as the timbers of ships being broken up provided good straight lengths of brine-pickled lumber at rock-bottom prices, always popular with builders – there are crucks, there are ties, there are Early English-style flat-headed archways, there is matchboard panelling. There aren't even that many tables and chairs: drinking is done either standing up, or perched on tall stools. It may not be a 17th-century city tavern. But it's an Edwardian Englishman's idea of what a 17th-century city tavern ought to be, which is the next best thing. It sells **Adnams Bitter**, **Harveys Sussex Best Bitter**, **Fuller's London Pride** and a guest beer. It opens all day during the week but closes at weekends. Lunches are available.

Turn left out of the pub and continue down Watling Street to Queen Victoria Street and fork right into Cornhill. Then turn right into St Michael's Alley for the **Jamaica Wine House** (5). Take only a few steps down St Michael's Alley and you are in a different world. It is, quite literally, Dickensian. Scrooge's counting house was in a court just like this, Mr Pickwick took up quarters in the George and Vulture, now a restaurant; and the shady lawyers of *The Pickwick Papers*, Dodson and Fogg, had chambers in Newman Court, thinly disguised as Freeman's Court, just across Cornhill. So it's an absolute certainty that Dickens knew the Jamaica, which was already old in his day. It was founded in 1652 as London's first coffee house and was re-established after the fire in the 1670s.

Coffee was a huge success among professional people and merchants of the 17th century and by the end of the century there were 3,000 coffee houses in London. This one started attracting merchants and others engaged in the West Indies trade and soon became known as the Jamaica. In 1869 the Jamaica was renamed the Jamaica Wine House and in 1892 it was rebuilt in contemporary tavern style. It's still a totally unspoilt and magnificent example of its period, divided into little compartments by polished mahogany partitions, with an oak bar and plain pine-plank bar-back, dark lino underfoot and tobacco-glazed pressed paper between big beams overhead. It's far too masculine for such a softening influence as upholstery to be permitted. On the hand pumps are **St Peter's Best** and **Golden** and **Draught Bass**. Food is served at lunchtimes. The pub opens all day from Mondays to Fridays but is closed at weekends.

Turn left out of the pub through St Michael's churchyard, go down Bell Inn Yard, cross Gracechurch Street, turn left and then right into Leadenhall Market. The existing market was designed by the City Corporation's architect, Horace Jones – the same man who built the markets at Smithfield and Billingsgate – and went up in 1881. It is the most glorious confection of decorative cast iron imaginable, and although it is now given over almost entirely to bars and restaurants, there are still two butchers and one fishmonger left in it.

Of the two pubs inside the market the **New Moon** (6) on the corner of the Gracechurch Street entrance, is the less well-known. And yet it's a magnificent pub with a ground-floor bar that is long and narrow, with a counter stretching down most of its length and a fine carved wooden bar-back behind. Overhead is a high, sombre ceiling, heavily beamed in the Jacobean style. The impression is of formality and grandeur, as opposed to the cosier ambience of the Lamb in the centre of the market. A bill found during a recent refurbishment and dated 18 August 1900 reveals that the pub was originally called the Half Moon. Steak and chips then would have set you back one shilling and three pence. You pay rather more than that for the pizzas now sold in the cellar bar with other dishes at lunchtimes. It opens all day Mondays to Fridays up to 10.30 pm but is closed on weekends. It sells **Brakspear Bitter**, **Boddingtons Bitter**, **Flowers IPA** and **Fuller's London Pride**.

Turn right out of the pub for the **Lamb Tavern** (7) by far the better-known of the market's two pubs and a very different proposition to the cavernous New Moon.

The first Lamb on the site was built in 1780 by a wine and spirits merchant named Pardy and was a proper inn. It was rebuilt, minus its letting rooms and outbuildings, along with the rest of the market and was a fine, ornate Victorian pub. It was always run as a free house, leased from the Corporation, but was taken over by Young's in 1985 and substantially remodelled in 1987. A good deal of original work remains – the tiling in the dive bar, for instance, and the ceramic depiction in the lobby of Wren inspecting his plans – and Young's made pub history by turning the upstairs lounge into the City's first smoke-free bar. But the decision to insert a mezzanine, reached by a spiral iron staircase, into the ground-floor saloon bar must have altered the character of the Lamb immensely. Instead of the grand bar with lofty ceiling that we still see in the New Moon, the Lamb is cosy and intimate. It sells **Young's Bitter**, **Special** and seasonal beers and food is served all day. It opens from 11 am to 9 pm during the week but closes at the weekend.

Return to the Gracechurch Street exit and turn left into Ship Tavern Passage and the **Swan** (8). It really is a tiny pub, a narrow sliver of a pub lining one side of an alleyway – one deep at the bar and the place is pretty well full, although there's a slightly larger area at the far end of the mahogany-panelled bar where three or four biggish people or half-a-dozen normal ones can at least breathe freely, if not gesticulate too animatedly.

Up the stairs with its green marble tiling, though, it's a different story. The lounge spans the alleyway and is therefore twice as wide as the tiny saloon; and even so this room isn't exactly cavernous. The upstairs lounge is a lovely room with its heavy tasselled drapes, red printed wallpaper, and big gilt-framed mirror, it could be the drawing-room of an Edwardian parsonage – albeit one from which someone had removed all the armchairs.

The Swan is one of the few outlets in the City for **Fuller's** excellent **Chiswick Bitter**, a former Champion Beer of Britain with an extremely sensible alcohol content of 3.5 per cent. This is not nearly as big a seller as the brewery's better-known and rather stronger **London Pride** which with others from the range is also sold, but regulars of the Swan will assure you that it's a far better lunchtime beer if you plan to do any work that afternoon. It opens all day Mondays to Fridays but is closed at weekends and serves lunches.

Turn left into Gracechurch Street and the Monument underground station (District and Circle lines) is across the road.

The Blackfriar, 174 Queen Victoria Street

THE WEDGE-SHAPED Blackfriar is unique. Built in 1875 and remodelled 25 or so years later, it would be a fairly straightforward Olde English pub with the usual black oak beams and small-paned leaded windows if it weren't for the astounding decorative scheme superimposed in 1902 by Henry Poole.

Poole was a leading figure in the Arts & Crafts Movement inspired by William Morris, and was master of the movement's governing body, the Art Workers' Guild, in 1906. He took as his theme the Dominican friary which had occupied the site in the Middle Ages, and decorated the whole place inside and out with the most incredible copper bas-reliefs of fat, jolly, and distinctly unspiritual friars engaged in various labours connected, in one way or another, with the pleasures of drink, all illustrated with trite aphorisms such as "Silence is Golden", "Wisdom is Rare", and "Industry is All".

If that was all Poole had done, it would have been extraordinary enough; but he didn't stop there. Surely testing the depths of his client's pocket to the limit, he smothered the interior in marble. The walls are covered in plaques of it. The mullions of the windows are sheathed with it. There are columns of it and carvings in it; and the whole ceiling of the secluded little snug at the back is vaulted with it, as if it were a side-chapel in some Byzantine basilica. (Check out the four light fittings in this snug: labelled Morn, Noon, Even and Night, each has a marble figure including the devil hanging upside down like a sleeping bat at Noon; but each also has its little bronze monk).

Then there are mirrors, mosaics, bronze gargoyles, stained-glass window-panes – every decorative trick conceivable in an explosion of exuberant, ebullient, effervescent, extravagant craftsmanship. It's a truly amazing feat, almost too good a thing for a mere pub. Indeed, the flippant tone of the decorations suggests that Poole might have thought as much himself. For all that, the Blackfriar is a major achievement and a landmark in the history of English decorative art.

'appy 'ampstead

*'Ladies who value their reputation have of late
avoided the wells and walks at Hampstead.'*   DANIEL DEFOE

*'Hampstead is the most delightful place for air
and scenery near London.'*   ROBERT LOUIS STEVENSON

Well into the 19th century, Hampstead was still a separate
village, with open fields dividing it from Camden Town.
Its Heath was a lung of greenery with its highest point,
although a mere 440 feet above sea-level, a good stiff walk
for a city-dweller who might never normally climb
anything higher than a few flights of stairs; and its springs
gave pure water, a rare commodity in the polluted city.
Today it has been swallowed up by London but retains a
certain village charm.

The crawl starts at Hampstead Station and finishes at
Chalk Farm which are both on the Edgware branch of the
Northern Line.

Turn right out of the station and cross Heath Street.
Holly Mount is directly opposite; follow it uphill and round
to the right to the **Holly Bush** (1). This is one of Hampstead's
landmark pubs, neglected and run down in the late 1990s
as the brewery which owned it, fiercely opposed by the
local community, tried and failed to get permission to turn
it into yet another chic café-bar. It would have been an
outrage for the Holly Bush has a character entirely its own.

It was originally the stable-block to the artist George
Romney's house, and is said to have been built in the 1640s.
The pub's unassuming exterior merges well into the
jumble of houses that fill the surrounding narrow streets
of the Mount; but step inside and its true character is
revealed. It is a perfectly preserved working-class ale house
of the 1860s, very spartan, all high-backed settles, bare
floorboards, matchboard-clad walls and smoke-stained
dark ceilings; but with bits and pieces of 1890s

ornamentation. The front bar has been left untouched, and a large room upstairs which was a dining room a century ago is a dining room once more, specialising in that one-time worker's staple, oysters, and other seafood. Oh, dogs are welcome and there are new loos.

Open 12–11 Monday–Saturday; 12–10.30 Sunday. Food served all day. Real ales: **Adnams Bitter** *and* **Broadside**, **Fuller's London Pride** *and guests* .

From the pub carry straight on and go down a set of steps to your left. Cross Heath Street, turn left, then right into New End to the **Duke of Hamilton** (2). This fairly large early Victorian back-street local is bright and cheerful and exceptionally comfortable in an Edwardian-parlour sort of way, with carpets rather than bare boards and upholstered benches rather than wooden ones, and plenty of light and colour. The bar-back has some nice engraved glass, and there are fireplaces at each end which show by their location how the pub was once divided. The pub has excellent beer and has been a regular entry in the *Good Beer Guide* for years. (It also used to have Oliver Reed as a regular: his picture hangs on the wall.)

Open 12–11; 12–10.30 Sunday. Bar snacks 12–2. Real ales: **Fuller's London Pride**, **ESB**, *and seasonal special; guest ale; draught Czech lager, traditional draught cider and 15 malt whiskies.*

Turn left out of the pub and walk straight down New End into New End Square passing the Hampstead Museum. Turn right into Flask Walk for the **Flask Tavern** (3), which is another working-class boozer much favoured by musicians. Like the Holly Bush, it's a no-frills two-roomed pub but with the odd ornamental flourish inserted to update it. There is decorative tile work on the façade, and a tiled dado in the public bar. In 1990 the pub was extended by the addition of a back bar and a conservatory-dining room, which remain an object lesson to developers in how to add new to old without jarring. There is pavement seating in summer.

Open all permitted hours. Food served 12–3 and 6–8.30 Tuesday–Friday; 12–4 and 6–8.30 Saturday; 12–4 Sunday and Monday. Real ales: **Young's** *range.*

Turn left out of the pub and then left again down Hampstead High Street and Rosslyn Hill. Turn left into Downshire Hill to the **Freemasons Arms** (4). The southern slopes of Hampstead are a very different proposition from the tangled, narrow knot of lanes and alleys in the old village with broad leafy avenues lined with elegant bow-fronted Regency villas and the handsome, spacious Freemasons is no humble working-class local.

The present pub was built in the 1930s, its early 19th-century predecessor having been found structurally unsound because a tributary of the River Fleet flowed under it and it was demolished. But the architects and builders of the new Freemasons did a worthy job which puts much of the pub design of the period (and, indeed, of today) to shame.

Outside, its clean lines and Regency windows complement its neighbours perfectly; and while inside it is actually a single big T-shaped room there's nothing remotely barn-like about it. Its three separate spaces are broken up by glazed pine screens, but with a rather incongruous quarry-tiled floor creating a unity. Children are welcomed; the ale is well-kept and there's even a London skittle alley where heavy cheeses of lignum vitae are not rolled at the hornbeam pins but hurled at them.

Open 12–11 (12–10.30 Sunday). Food served 12–10.
Real ales: **Tetley Bitter**, **Draught Bass**.

Turn left out of the pub and right into South End Road. Keats's House (he lived here from 1818 to 1820) is to the right in Keats Grove and is open to the public. Return to South End Road; turn right and then left into South Hill Park for the **Magdala** (5).

First, its name: Magdala was an Ethiopian fort that Robert Napier destroyed in 1868 – he got raised to the peerage for it, too, as Lord Napier of Magdala and his victory is memorialised by a singularly hideous ceramic landscape in the lobby. This big and rather gaunt pub, with little decoration other than the green marble columns dividing the upper-storey Venetian windows – is far more famous as the scene on Easter Sunday 1955 of the shooting by Ruth Ellis of her abusive and faithless lover and that she was the last woman to be hanged in Britain. No attempt is made these days to capitalise on this and instead, the Magdala was reinvented as rather a smart, understated, two-room pub, very cool and light and airy, with pale panelled walls and pictures of old Hampstead. There's a calm and uncluttered lounge bar, and a bigger room with French windows opening on to a pleasant garden. In the rather unlovely surroundings of south Hampstead, the Magdala is something of an oasis.

Open all permitted hours. Food served 12–3, 6.30–10 Monday–Friday; 12–10 Saturday; 12–9.30 Sunday. Real ales: **Greene King IPA, Fuller's London Pride**.

Cross South End Square and turn right up Pond Street, then left down Haverstock Hill. Cross Haverstock Hill and turn right into England's Lane and on the right is the **Washington** (6). This stately pub, originally a hotel, has a fascia of rusticated quoins, huge sash windows, and black marble columns with fancy gold-painted capitals.

If the pub's exterior is of the classically-minded mid-19th century, its interior is triumphantly 1890s. There are mirrors of engraved glass, and another painted with a riverbank scene; there is a partition of pitch-pine and acid-etched glass screening the public bar; there is a magnificent plaster ceiling painted dark green, with equally ornate cornices picked out in cream and there are heavy drapes framing the big sash windows.

The Washington is named, according to a local researcher, not after George Washington but after the Sussex village where the developer originally came from.

Open 10–11 Monday–Friday; 12–10.30 Sunday. Food 10–10 Monday–Friday; 12–10 Sunday. Real ales: **Tetley Burton Ale, Draught Bass, Greene King IPA, Adnams Bitter, Fuller's London Pride**.

Return to Haverstock Hill and turn right for the **Sir Richard Steele** (7). What a fantastic pub to end the walk with! Big and plain from outside, the interior of this 1870s street-corner pub is a treasure-trove of bric-à-brac collected over the years – some of it donated by customers – and placed with wit and aplomb. The place is festooned with prints, photographs, drawings, paintings, stone busts, typewriters, mincers, irons, sewing machines, clocks, toys, enamel advertisements, railway signs, mirrors, bottles, books by the thousand – even a child's dog-cart hanging from the ceiling over a fireplace. This is bric-à-brac with attitude.

Now look at the ceiling. It's a Renaissance pastiche of heroic proportions, skilfully and laboriously painted by an enterprising young artist who worked at it for over three months, erecting his scaffolding once the regulars had departed and toiling on through the night until their return. Many of them are actually in it, as are several of the politicians who were in the news at the time. It all gives style and humour to a pub which would probably have been scraped out and given a standard pattern-book refurbishment if it had been owned by some big brewery or pub company rather than by a private individual with a well-developed sense of the bizarre. It was all opened out in the 1960s but two cosy little snugs were fortunately left at the back.

The pub is named after the journalist and playwright Sir Richard Steele who co-founded both the *Tatler* and the *Spectator* and who lived nearby. A fantastic stained-glass window dedicated to him dating from 1900 is in a corner of the pub.

Open all permitted hours. No food. Real ales: **Greene King IPA** *and* **Old Speckled Hen, Flowers Original, Adnams Bitter**.

Turn right out of the pub and continue down Haverstock Hill to Chalk Farm Station.

Kensington

THE PUBS OF KENSINGTON REFLECT, for the most part, the district's suburban tranquillity. Notting Hill Gate and Kensington High Street may be full of hideous modern style bars and restaurants where the food is as overpriced as it is over-hyped; but away from the main roads are quiet residential enclaves, with unfussy pubs to match.

You start at Notting Hill Gate tube station, walk eastwards along the southern side of Notting Hill Gate for a few yards, then turn right and walk down Kensington Church Street to the **Churchill Arms** (1). Originally called the Marlborough after John Churchill, Duke of Marlborough, who led Britain to victory in the War of the Spanish Succession, this pleasantly scruffy mid-Victorian pub was renamed after the celebrated member of a cadet branch of the family did his country the same favour in the Second World War.

It's a large pub, with all the original partitions knocked out to create one big horseshoe-shaped lounge which is all wood-panelled. Naturally enough, there are paintings, photographs and busts of Churchill himself; but whoever has amassed this astonishing collection of bits and pieces has not been able to stop there. There's a picture-gallery boasting every Prime Minister from Robert Walpole to Harold Wilson with Churchill as a centrepiece and there are enough stoneware flagons, copper jugs, brass buckets and wicker creels to revive the *Old Curiosity Shop*, and Heaven knows what beside. Bric-à-brac has run riot over the years. At the back, however, the mood changes utterly. A recently-added conservatory, hung with cool fronds of foliage, doubles as a restaurant where Thai food is an evening speciality. It sells the **Fuller's** range of real ales. It opens all day, every day and food is served every lunchtime and evenings except Sunday evening.

Turn right and continue down Church Street for the **Catherine Wheel** (2). Designed in 1870 the pub dominates its corner site just off Kensington High Street, its wide ground-floor façade provided with a handsome brown marble fascia, and inside its ceiling, now painted bottle-green, is unusually high. But it's not actually a very big pub at all, and it's hard to imagine what it must have been like when – as it undoubtedly originally was – it was partitioned into two or three rooms. Sadly, successive refurbishments have left few clues other than a single pleasant fireplace with a surround of red tiles and a fine cut-glass mirror above. Still, it's a pleasant and well-situated retreat from the hustle and bustle of Kensington High Street. The name, incidentally, is usually taken as referring either to the Turner's Company, which uses a Catherine Wheel in its coat of arms, or to the Order of St Catherine, which protected pilgrims in Crusader times and whose symbol was therefore associated with travel in general. It was a common name among coaching inns and posting houses, so perhaps Williams's Catherine Wheel replaced an earlier posting house on the site. Real ales on the bar are **Adnams Bitter**, **Fuller's London Pride** and changing guests. It opens all day and provides bar meals up to 6 pm and sandwiches after that from Mondays to Saturdays and roast dinners all day Sundays.

Go into Kensington High Street, turn left, then cross the road opposite Barker's and turn right down Young Street alongside the store for the **Greyhound** (3), in Kensington Square. Almost opposite Thackeray's house, the Greyhound the novelist knew was a humble workingman's boozer where an old custom was carried on. It was common, in the 19th century, for labourers to down tools at lunchtime and go and buy a chop or a steak, which a friendly publican would grill for them for nothing on condition that they bought a pot or two of beer to wash it down with. We know that this custom was observed at the Greyhound because *Licensing World* in 1898 recorded complaints that there would be no such facility when it was pulled down and rebuilt.

The new Greyhound, which opened in 1899, was a very much smarter emporium, noted for its glasswork. When two full-sized billiard tables were installed it rapidly became a centre for the game where the stars of the day such as Joe and Fred Davies would often play. All this came to an end one night in 1979, when a gas explosion destroyed the pub in its entirety and, luckily, no-one was in at the time. The façade was rebuilt as before, but the interior is very different, comprising not much more than a single enormous room, comfortable enough if a trifle anonymous, with a low ceiling which makes the whole place appear rather gloomy. The situation, however, could hardly be better: although not more than 200 yards from Kensington High Street, Kensington Square is a calm green oasis of modest but very pleasant 18th-century houses. It's no wonder that the philosopher John Stuart Mill, the actress Mrs Patrick Campbell, and the Pre-Raphaelite painter Edward Burne-Jones all chose to live in it. **Theakston Best Bitter** and **Courage Directors** are on the hand pumps. It opens through the day, all week and meals are served from noon to 10 pm.

Stroll round Kensington Square, returning to Kensington High Street from Derry Street. Turn left and go along until you come to Allen Street, then turn left for the **Britannia** (4).

This charming and unpretentious little pub, with its little public bar partitioned off from the wood-panelled lounge, was once the tap for William Wells's Britannia Brewery – indeed, the old brewery stable yard is now the pub's conservatory. Both brewery and pub were built in 1834, shortly after the area, previously market gardens, had been developed. The brewery never seems to have done well and it was bought along with its two pubs, by Young's in 1924 and soon demolished. The existing frontage and interior panelling actually date only to 1960, when the pub was remodelled and extended, but such are their simplicity that they are effectively timeless – and proof that modern design can be as good as any. It's still very much a locals' pub – although the locals today are very much grander than they were when the district was developed – with the emphasis on quality: it is one of only a couple of dozen or so pubs across the nation to have appeared in every single edition of the Campaign for Real Ale's *Good Beer Guide* since the first edition in 1974. It opens from 11 am to 11 pm from Mondays to Saturdays and from noon to 10.30 pm on Sundays. Bar food is served all day and there is a separate restaurant. A full range of **Young's** beers is sold.

Continue south down Allen Street and turn right into Abingdon Villas; cross Earl's Court Road and cut down Earl's Walk beside the Police Station. Turn right into Edwardes Square and the **Scarsdale Arms** (5) which has undergone a thorough revamp, apparently comparatively recently, and is none the worse for it. All the original partitions have gone, leaving a square island bar projecting into a single large room. But skilful design has created three quite distinct spaces. On the left as you enter is a bistro-like dining area with walls of whitewashed brick; the lobby area retains its pubby feel thanks to a predominance of bare woodwork; while to the right is a second dining area with a more formal atmosphere created by a dark green and red colour scheme, with a few large, well-chosen paintings in heavy gilt frames and discreet wall lighting.

This is a pub which, with its imaginative selection of real ales – **Courage Directors**, **Marston's Pedigree**, **Greene King Old Speckled Hen** and two guest ales from micro-breweries – its fine wines, its Bloody Maries made to a secret house recipe, and its excellent food, suits its neighbourhood very well. Kensington High Street is a mere 100 yards away, with all its noise, fumes, and traffic, but Edwardes Square remains leafy, tranquil, and private. A famous resident of recent years was a very private man who must have appreciated its apparent seclusion: Frankie Howerd, the comedian, lived in the Square from 1966 until his death in 1992. It is open all day, all week and bar food is served all the time although there is a full menu only at lunchtimes and up to 10 pm.

Turn right out of the pub and immediately left. Walk round the south and west sides of Edwardes Square into Kensington High Street; cross it; turn left, then right into Addison Road and immediately right into Holland Park Road. Tucked away down a side street in a modest red-brick townhouse, is the delightful LEIGHTON HOUSE MUSEUM, for 30 years home to the painter, Lord Frederick Leighton. It became a private museum after his death in 1896. Sadly, his personal collection had to be sold on his death but over the years the house has been patiently restocked, and it is a wonderful surprise to find such a magnificent collection in such an unlikely location. It opens Mondays to Thursdays from 11 am to 5.30 pm.

Continue along Holland Park Road. Turn right at the end, then left along Kensington High Street turning left into Phillimore Gardens and then right into Stafford Terrace for LINLEY SAMBOURNE HOUSE a tall Georgian terraced house that was the home of the eponymous cartoonist and illustrator until his death in 1910. It is presented to the public as he left it, decorated in the aesthetic manner complete with William Morris wallpaper, hung with works by well-known artists of the period as well as Sambourne's collection of oriental ceramics. It is open to the general public at weekends but visits must be booked (020 7602 3316).

Continue along Stafford Terrace. Turn right at the end into Argyll Road, then left and immediately left again into Campden Hill Road. Continue north and cross over for the **Windsor Castle** (6).

This is a pub to make a patriot and a nationalist of anyone, for it enshrines so many of the virtues we English like in our pubs. The beers – **Draught Bass** and **Fuller's London Pride** are well-kept; the food ranges from simple but excellent snacks up to full-blown gourmet extravagances; and the decor and the atmosphere, while utterly unspoilt and in some regards even basic, are the essence of pub distilled. The front bar is divided into three well-lived in areas, all bare boards, wooden panels, and high-backed settles; while the only access to the other two bars is by midget hatchways through the partitions. Each of these snugs actually has its own street door, but these are evidently never used. Beyond lies a large and pleasant stone-floored courtyard with a shady plane tree, gas heating, and plenty of tables and benches. It opens every day at noon and through the day with food served up to 10 pm.

Continue along Campden Hill Road and turn right into Kensington Place and then left into Hillgate Street for the **Hillgate** (7). The area was laid out in the 1840s and '50s on the site of a notorious slum by a family of builders and local landowners called Johnson, one of whose members became Lord Mayor of London in 1846. Hillgate Street was originally Johnson Street, and the Hillgate was the Johnson Arms when it was built in 1854. And although so much has changed this is still a discreet residential area, with small local shops and unpretentious restaurants. The two-bar Hillgate is also still a genuinely local pub. Visit in the early afternoon, when the lunchtime trade has died down, and you'll even find elderly working-class drinkers here, villagers all their lives, gossiping in genuine working-class accents about nothing very much. There's nothing particularly special about the Hillgate, it has to be said: it has no history to speak of, and the architecture is workaday; but therein lies its appeal. It's just a bloody good little boozer with plain food and excellent beer – if only there were more like it. Real ales on the bar are **Greene King IPA** and **Abbot**, **Shepherd Neame Spitfire** and **Charles Wells Bombardier**. Bar food is served up to 3 pm and from 6 pm to 9 pm. The pub opens all day.

Continue along Hillgate Street and turn right into Notting Hill Gate to where the crawl started.

Wandsworth
Around Britain's oldest brewery

BEER HAS BEEN BREWED continuously since the 16th century on the site of **Young's Ram Brewery** at the corner of Wandsworth High Street and what is now Ram Street. Running under the road is the River Wandle which, during the Industrial Revolution, became the most worked river in the country. For more than a 100 years a canal also ran from the Thames to the back of the brewery site. The canal basin was also a wharf for the horse-drawn Surrey Iron Railway which connected the Thames with Croydon and Merstham during the first half of the 19th century.

The 20th century saw the canal filled in, the remaining mills closed and the development of Wandsworth progressively dictated by the volume of road traffic passing through it. But the Ram Brewery, first acquired by Charles Young and Anthony Bainbridge in 1831, continues to dominate the town centre and horse-power still hauls beer to the nearest Young's pubs.

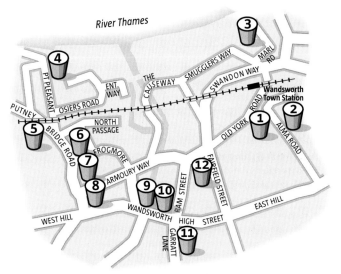

Wandsworth – Around Britain's oldest brewery

The Thames riverside area either side of the Wandle delta is now being redeveloped. Wandsworth is looking up, which is good news for its abundant legacy of pubs and, while you would expect there to be a predominance of Young's pubs, there is also a fine selection of other beers from other breweries.

Our crawl is anticlockwise starting and finishing at Wandsworth Town, the next station to Clapham Junction, which is served by stopping trains every quarter hour between Waterloo and Richmond or Hounslow. Opposite the station entrance, on the other side of Old York Road is the **Alma** (1), a large tile-fronted Victorian corner pub, its name commemorating the Crimean War battle in 1854. Sensitive renovation in 1987 saw the restoration of many original features including a decorative plaster frieze in the restaurant area. It serves the full range of **Young's** draught beers: **Bitter**, **Special**, the seasonal **Winter Warmer** or **Waggle Dance** (the strong, honey beer originated by Wards).

This traditional but stylish pub has a continental feel and may be worth a return visit at the end of the day.

On leaving, turn right into Podmore Road, staying south of the railway then cross Alma Road and across Ballantine Street is the **Tonsley Tup** (2), which until recently was called the Royal Standard. It is a small, back-street local, tastefully refurbished in 2001 and now serving **Greene King IPA**.

Carry on along Podmore Road until you reach its junction with Bramford Road on the right. To the left under the railway arch is now a direct walk to the next pub: follow the footpath between the fenced greens, cross the busy Swandon Way at the pedestrian crossing and cut through the car park, by the east wall of McDonald's. Carry straight on down Jews Row and at the end, on the left, is the **Ship** (3) an old inn first leased by Young's in 1832. Surrounding cottages have been demolished to allow an open view of the Thames. The saloon bar has been extended towards the river by a conservatory and restaurant. A separate south-facing door leads into a time warp – a small, quiet, corner public bar with an adjoining room.

From the public bar entrance, turn right up the westward limb of Jews Row, walk through into the Riverside West complex then turn left, away from the Thames, past the Outback Steak House and right into Smugglers Way. Stay on the north side of the road, passing the refuse tip, and then carry straight on into the Causeway. Turn right continuing over a new footbridge that takes you over Bell Lane Creek and into Enterprise Way, the easterly cul-de-sac of a small industrial estate north of the railway. Turn left and follow Osiers Road, parallel to the railway embankment, then turn right at the end into Point Pleasant.

Towards the end of Point Pleasant, adjoining a derelict warehouse on the right is an unexpected delight. The **Cat's Back** (4) (meaning 'the cat is back') is a privately-owned free house, dimly lit with a real fire, homely old furniture, original paintings, an attractive modern stained-glass window behind the bar and all sorts of strange artefacts. Up to four real ales may be available including at least one from the **Eccleshall Brewery's Slaters** range and one from **O'Hanlon's** which might be **Port Stout**. The pub was renamed in the 1990s to celebrate the return of a much loved (and now sadly missed) feline after a period of absence.

Retrace your steps along Point Pleasant, and continue under the railway bridge into Putney Bridge Road. To the left and across the road is a convivial **Young's** pub, the **Queen Adelaide** (5), named in the 1830s after King William IV's Queen. The pub has a large garden in which barbecues are held in the summer. Enjoy a peaceful, tasty pint of **Bitter**, **Special** or the seasonal beer.

Cross over to the other side of Putney Bridge Road and continue to the right (away from the river) past the *Hop Pole* (6) which is owned by **Shepherd Neame**. Continue, passing Frogmore, which is a route back to Wandsworth Town Station. Young's smallest pub, the *Wheatsheaf* (7), follows, then cross Armoury Way carefully and continue the short distance into Wandsworth High Street. On the corner is the **Rose and Crown** (8), restored by Wetherspoon to its original name and offering a range of beers which usually includes a welcome choice of two guest beers from micro-breweries. There is no canned music or fruit machines.

Go left again, eastwards along Wandsworth High Street, and wait for a break in the stream of one way traffic into Wandsworth Plain and on the corner, ahead of you, is the **King's Arms** (9), a spacious, warm and welcoming 18th-century pub bought by Young and Bainbridge from Lord Spencer in 1836. Behind the pub which is opposite the brewery is a large, secluded and prize-winning garden, running down to the Wandle. It sells the **Young's** standard range of beers.

Cross the Wandle and pass the main entrance to the brewery. Beyond is the *Brewery Tap* (10), originally called the Ram but used nowadays as Young's visitor centre and open only from 11.30 am to 5.30 pm on Mondays to Fridays and from 12 noon to 5 pm on Saturdays. The former public bar on the corner is now the brewery shop. Booking is advised for brewery trips, which usually start at 10 am, 12 noon, 2 pm and 4 pm. Telephone 020 8875 7005.

Close by on the opposite corner is the **Spread Eagle** (11) which retains its Victorian entrance archway over the pavement. This was another 1836 purchase and in its day it was an important coaching inn which accommodated a range of business and civic functions, including the local magistrates' courts. This popular, stately, two-bar pub with fine mirrors, ornate glass and mahogany partitions serves **Young's Bitter**, **Special** and seasonal beers and opens all permitted hours.

Cross back over Wandsworth High Street and head down Ram Street alongside the brewery. Before Ram Street joins Armoury Way, a plaque on the wall records the operation of the Surrey Iron Railway. Cross over here and turn right into Barchard Street and at the far end on the left at the corner of Fairfield Street, is a local gem, the **Grapes** (12). This small, charming, wood-panelled, early 19th-century pub with an award-winning garden has been a regular *Good Beer Guide* entry in recent years. **Young's Bitter** and **Special** are the two beers available.

On leaving turn left into Fairfield Street, then right at the junction into Old York Road which leads back to the station.

North West England

THIS DIVERSE REGION stretches from the edge of the Lake District to North Wales and is protected from the rest of England – and in particular Yorkshire – by the Pennine Chain also known as the 'black stump'. It has everything: from smart Cheshire towns, an industrial Lancastrian heartland, the flat fields of the Fylde, boisterous seaside resorts and rolling hilly, agricultural meadowland.

Lancashire was, of course, the birthplace of the cotton industry and it remains important although it has declined along with coal and shipbuilding. However, the resorts of Blackpool, Morecambe and Southport remain as popular as ever to the *hoi polloi* of the north.

Manchester, in particular, is famous for brewing with a clutch of medium sized independent breweries – Robinson's, Lees, Hydes, Holt – all producing excellent beers. Add to these other regional brewers and 30 thriving micros and you have a very healthy beer scene complemented by many fine pubs.

There is a variety of crawls taking you from Manchester's N/4 delights to a traditional village stroll, a raucous excursion around Blackpool and a bus run into the Pennines.

Blackpool

There's a seaside place called Blackpool
That's noted for fresh air and fun.

ALBERT AND THE LION

BLACKPOOL is Britain's premier seaside resort and is tremendously popular particularly in high summer. What does it have to offer to claim such predominance? Seven miles of sands, a tramway system that stretches 12 miles along the coast to Fleetwood, a 518 foot high tower, fantastic illuminations, the Golden Mile and the Pleasure Beach. And much, much more including some great pubs. This crawl starts in the suburbs and fringes the town centre to avoid most of the large crowds and it picks out the less crowded but nevertheless better quality pubs than those along and near the Promenade. But remember, this is Blackpool and Blackpool is uncompromisingly brash and noisy.

If you start at the railway or bus stations which are next to each other take a No 2 bus (destination Poulton) and ask to be dropped off at the **Number 4 and Freemasons** (1) at the junction of Layton Road and Newton Drive. This pleasant, smart, 1930s pub is a short stroll from Stanley Park and about a mile from the seafront. It has a large split-level lounge and a separate bar with pool and darts. The small forecourt area has picnic benches. The pub opens all day from 12 noon and **Thwaites Bitter** is on the hand pulls. Evening meals are served until 7 pm – look for the landlord's specials on the GM-free menu. Music and younger drinkers predominate in the evenings.
The car park is shared with the adjoining fitness centre.

Walk along Newton Drive towards the town centre and after crossing a main road turn left into Liverpool Road for the **Raikes Hall Hotel** (2) another pub that opens all day from noon. It sells **Draught Bass** and guest beers and meals are served up to 8 pm (7 pm on Sundays). This Grade II listed building dates from 1760 and from 1871 to 1901 was at the heart of Raikes Hall Gardens which offered lakes, theatres,

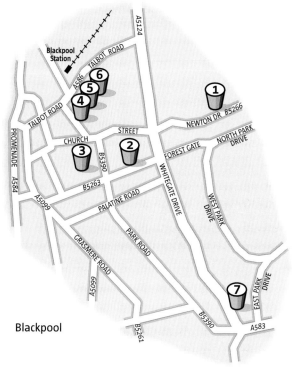

Blackpool

horse racing and a football ground. One large L-shaped room has lounge and bar areas. Picnic benches overlook the pub's own bowling green and provide a pleasant outdoor alternative. The first floor has a smart reception room for hire and displays a framed 1888 map of the gardens.

Retrace your steps and turn left into Church Street and head towards the town centre and after approximately 600 yards on the left is the **Blue Room** (3) which sells **Boddingtons Bitter**, **Fuller's London Pride**, **Greene King Abbot**, **Taylor Landlord** and guest beers. This busy, sometimes noisy, town-centre pub has recently reverted to its original name, having previously been called the Stanley Beer Engine. Newly painted and double-glazed, this popular pub offers food from 11 am to 5 pm. There are two pool tables, pinball and quiz machines.

Cross over into King Street which leads into Cookson Street and turn right at the end. Situated close to the railway and bus stations on Talbot Road is the **Wheatsheaf** (4). It is a delightfully down-to-earth, characterful boozer with collections of flags, pictures, mannequins and giant fish. Real fires are lit from autumn through to spring and add to the homely atmosphere. The lounge has a chandelier and the uncarpeted area a pool table and another collection – of wartime posters. There is also a small patio area that is used for barbecues. **Theakston Mild**, **Best Bitter**, **Old Peculier** and guest beers are sold and food is served all day up to 8 pm. Tuesdays are piano nights.

A few doors further on is the **Ramsden Arms Hotel** (5) once owned by the eponymous and long-dead Yorkshire brewery. The interior is oak-panelled, there are coal fires in winter and there is an interesting collection of mugs. **Boddingtons Bitter**, **Marston's Pedigree**, **Tetley Burton Ale** and **Bitter** and a guest beer are on the pumps. Accommodation is available (01253 623215).

Carry on for 100 yards or so to the **New Road Inn** (6) which is opposite the Mecca bingo. This small three-roomed town-centre pub is the first **Jennings** house in Blackpool and sells **Cumberland Ale** and **Sneck Lifter**. It has been recently redecorated throughout. The front room is dominated by the sweeping curved bar and features posters of 1930s passenger liners. Sometimes the music is quite loud and DJ nights may not be to all tastes, but the cask ale is amongst the cheapest in town. The pub provides bed and breakfast (01253 752666).

It is a short walk back to the two stations. If, however, you wish to continue this crawl to a splendid pub just out of town then catch a No 14 bus from the bus station headed for St Anne's and ask to be put off at the **Saddle** (7) in Whitegate Drive. This is Blackpool's oldest inn dating from 1770. There is a main bar and two side rooms, one wood-panelled with pictures of sporting heroes and the other, which has a real fire, acts as a no-smoking dining room at lunchtimes. There is a large, pleasant patio for summer drinking. It sells **Draught Bass**, **Hancock's HB**, **Worthington's Bitter** and guest beers.

Croston

CROSTON is a pleasant Lancashire village with the River Yarrow flowing through it. At one time there were 13 pubs here. Five miles away is the Martin Mere Wildfowl and Wetlands Centre so this crawl might appeal to twitchers with a thirst. There are rail links with Preston and Ormskirk and it is ten miles from the seaside resort of Southport. The village is twinned with Azay-le-Rideau in France's Loire Valley and international boules matches take place regularly between the two. The five pubs on this crawl are close together and serve 18 real ales between them which make for an excellent leisurely walkabout that is ideal for an evening out.

There are currently 12 trains a day in each direction with the last train back to Preston at 10.28 pm, arriving there at 10.45 pm. There is no service on Sundays. There is a bus service from Preston via Leyland (service 112) with the last bus back at 8.26 pm during the week and at 9.26 pm on Saturdays and just a skeleton service on Sundays. From Chorley, service C7 is a regular service during the day but there is only one bus back in the evening at 9.27 pm. There are also buses from Southport.

The visit starts at the white-fronted **Lord Nelson** (1) a former farmhouse in the centre of the village, set back from the main road and overlooking the green. This is the oldest pub in Croston and once belonged to Higsons of Liverpool but it has passed through several owners since then. Higsons beers, sadly, are no more. On the hand pumps are **Boddingtons Bitter**, **Robinson's Best Bitter**, **Worthington's Bitter**, **Jennings Cumberland Ale** and **Greene King IPA**. A single bar serves separate, cosy rooms and there are three real fires – one of which was once the original farmhouse cooking range. Snacks are available and there is occasional entertainment but no canned music. It is one of several pubs in the village that has a boules pitch.

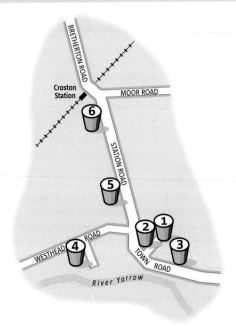

From here move to the **Wheatsheaf** (2), which is back on the main road within sight of the Lord Nelson. The quiet bar is part of a high quality restaurant and drinkers are made most welcome. The real ales on sale are **Boddingtons Bitter**, **Taylor Landlord**, **Greene King Abbot** and **Old Speckled Hen**, **Boggart Hole Clough Dark Side**, and another guest ale from a micro-brewery.

The **Grapes** (3) is an old pub across the road from the River Yarrow and next door to the historic church and Bushells House, which caters for 'distressed gentlefolk'. It is a charming low-beamed community pub with a large open fire in the centre of the main drinking area; there are several rooms and a separate dining area. On the hand pumps are **Boddingtons Bitter**, **Taylor Landlord**, and two guest beers such as **Coach House Dick Turpin**, **Khean All Rounder**, usually from micro-breweries. Food served includes specialities made with local produce such as Goosnargh duck. It has a bowling green.

The **Black Horse** (4), in Westhead Road at the south end of the village, is a large, handsome, solidly-built Victorian, village pub with open bar areas, open fires, a games room with hatch, a front snug and outside drinking and children's play areas. On sale are **John Smith's Bitter**, **Moorhouses Premier**, **Pendle Witches Brew** and **Black Cat**, **Charles Wells Bombardier**, **Jennings Cumberland Ale**, **Phoenix Arizona** and **Black Sheep Best Bitter** with occasional guest beers. There is a no-smoking dining room to the rear where good value food is served all lunchtimes and evenings except Mondays. The pub is big into crown green bowls and boules.

The **Crown** (5) in Station Road is an ivy-clad, brick-built **Thwaites** tied house and has three of their excellent cask beers on sale: **Mild**, **Original Bitter** and a seasonal ale. The pub has been recently refurbished with no adverse changes. It is very friendly and comfortable with an oak-beamed lounge bar divided into several separate areas and a public bar and games room. There is also a delightful garden with a boules pitch. It opens all day and good value lunches are served.

The _de Trafford Arms_ (6) close to the railway station currently sells no real ale and is mainly an eating establishment although there was a time when it sold beers from J W Lees of Middleton Junction.

Lancashire's rural bus trail

COOPERATION BETWEEN CAMRA and Lancashire County Council has resulted in the production of a leaflet outlining a pub trail from the busy county town of Preston to the pretty Pennine village of Chipping passing through other attractive villages and the small market town of Longridge. This crawl is based on pubs in the leaflet. Most of the pubs called at are at bus stops or within easy walking distance of one. The bus services are frequent, running well into the late evening but a timetable is advisable as there are route variations. Copies of the leaflet *Lancashire's Rural Ale Trail* and a full timetable (leaflet 103) can be obtained from Traveline on 0870 608 2608.

Most of the services start at Preston bus station although the C2 service to Longridge runs at half past the hour up to 6.30 pm from Lancaster Road.

The first stop is in Preston's northern suburb of Fulwood at the **Anderton Arms** (1) in Longsands Lane. But check, for some bus services do not go into Fulwood. This is a large, well-furnished and comfortable pub where the prices tend to reflect the decor. **Tetley Bitter** is the regular hand pulled beer with two guest ales from a rotating list. There is also an extensive wine list. The pub opens all day and food is served up to 10 pm. It has a no-smoking area and quiet areas and occasional live entertainment.

Move on to Grimsargh for the **Plough** (2) in Preston Road where the 104 service stops outside the pub. It is multi-roomed, smart and comfortable, welcomes children and opens all permitted hours. On the hand pumps are **Theakston Best Bitter** and two guest beers from the Scottish and Newcastle list. Meals are served at lunchtimes and in the early evenings.

It is a short run to Alston and on the main road is the **White Bull** (3) a **Thwaites** pub selling **Original Bitter** and **Lancaster Bomber** on hand pumps. It is a deceptively large

Lancashire's rural bus trail

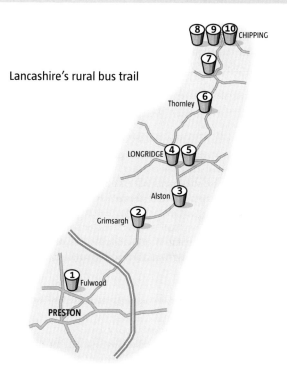

pub that has recently been extended with a large beer garden added. There is a games room. It opens all day and serves good value meals at lunchtimes and in the evenings up to 9 pm except on Mondays.

In less than five minutes you will be in the pleasant market town of Longridge nestling under the eponymous fell. The famous Longridge Field Day in mid-June attracts visitors from all over Lancashire. It is a procession with Morris Dance, brass bands, jazz and many other attractions and it raises lots of money for local charities. It is a friendly town with several pubs and the two selected have featured in the *Good Beer Guide*.

Alight at Severn Close bus stop for the **Old Oak** (4) in Preston Road. This is a welcoming community local with wooden settles and a real fire in the comfortable lounge.

95

There is also a games room and outside tables in summer. One area is no-smoking when lunches are served. On the taps are **Theakston Mild** and **Best Bitter**, **Charles Wells Bombardier** and two constantly-changing guest beers often from local small breweries. There is an old-fashioned feel about Sunday evenings with singalongs to the piano and waiter service. The pub has its own beer appreciation society and organises some amusing competitions. It opens from 12 noon every day.

Near the Market Square bus stop is the **White Bull Hotel** (5) in Higher Road. This 18th-century stone-built pub has quite a history that is shown on a board at the entrance. It has its quiet periods during the week but gets busy at the weekends. Nevertheless its four areas cater for all tastes and even include a bottle bar. **M&B Mild**, **Worthington's Bitter** and at least two guest beers are on the hand pulls. The pub opens at 5 pm on Mondays, it closes during the afternoons on Tuesdays and Wednesdays, and is open all day from 12 noon Thursdays to Sundays when food is served up to 7 pm. An unusual architectural feature is the stained-glass leaded-light window that was covered over with cement for many years.

It is a five-minute run to the **Derby Arms** (6) on the main road at Thornley. This free house serves quality food and runs popular themed nights in its restaurant – seafood is a speciality. It dates from the 18th century and was formerly a coaching inn. **Greenalls Bitter** and **Marston's Pedigree** are on the hand pulls. In the small tap room there is an interesting collection of ties. The pub closes during the afternoons.

The next bus stop is at the **Dog and Partridge** (7) in Hesketh Lane about a mile from Chipping. Some of the building dates from 1515 and in the past it has been named the Cliviger and the Green Man. This is very much an eating house promoting English food but well-kept **Tetley Mild** and **Bitter** and a regularly-changing guest ale are on the hand pumps. Bar meals are served at lunchtimes and in the evenings and the restaurant opens at weekends. All dining areas are no-smoking. It closes in the afternoons except on Sundays when it opens all day from noon. Children are welcome.

Chipping, which in old English means market, is an ancient village with stone-built houses and cobbled streets.

It is attractively situated in the Trough of Bowland and has won many 'best-kept village' competitions over the years. The post office claims to be the oldest continually used shop in England. There are three pubs all in the centre of the village, and while the beer selection is not wide they are all worth a visit.

Start at the **Tillotson's Arms** (8) in Talbot Street where **Boddingtons Bitter** and **Flowers IPA** are on the hand pumps. This popular, traditional local closes in the afternoons except on Sundays and bank holidays when it is open all day. There is no lunchtime opening on Mondays except bank holidays. Quite simple really. Food is served at all sessions up to 8.30 pm.

Also in Talbot Street is the **Talbot** (9) a popular pub with several rooms including one dedicated to games. It closes in the afternoons. Meals are served up to 9 pm with children welcome in the dining area. Dogs are welcome in the snug. On the hand pumps are **Boddingtons Bitter**, **Flowers IPA** and a guest beer that is frequently **Black Sheep Best Bitter**. There is regular live entertainment.

The final call is at the **Sun Inn** (10) in Windy Street that sells **Boddingtons Bitter** and **Taylor Landlord** and a guest beer. This is a popular stone-built pub which opens all day but serves meals only at lunchtimes – the range of unusual pies is not to be missed. It is reputedly haunted by the ghost of a girl who worked at the pub, was jilted and committed suicide.

It is worth noting that the last bus from Chipping on Mondays to Wednesdays is at 6.30 pm and at 6.27 pm on Sundays but as late as 10.55 pm from Thursdays to Saturdays.

Manchester's Northern Quarter

MANCHESTER was Britain's first great industrial city built on coal and cotton and self-confidence. It was the nation's centre of radical thought and political action. Much remains of its Victorian self-esteem but a lot has vanished in a devastation of municipal and corporate vandalism. The decline of what is now known as the Northern Quarter is, however, set to be reversed and there are obvious signs of renewal particularly in the Smithfield area. There is a bustling wholesale clothing trade and some of the best Indian cafés in the city. But what the Northern Quarter is best known for is some fine pubs and probably the best choice of real ale in the world.

Start from Victoria Station, a convenient spot for trains, trams and buses. Head north up Corporation Street, turning left under the railway to Red Bank. Walk up to Honey Street and the **Queen's Arms** (1) that overlooks the Irk Valley. It will take about 15 minutes. This friendly pub which retains its Empress Brewery façade serves **Phoenix Bantam**, **Taylor Landlord**, guest beers and a selection of Belgian draught and bottled beers. It opens all day, every day, from 12 noon and good meals are served until 8 pm. It is popular with families and has a children's play area and good views of the city's changing skyline.

Retrace your steps down Red Bank and turn left along Roger Street crossing the River Irk by the footbridge. Take Gould Street and at the junction with Rochdale Road is the **Marble Arch** (2). It opens all day from 11.30 am and from 12 noon on Sundays. This brew-pub now produces and sells fully organic (and vegan) beers with such interesting names as **Marble Manchester Bitter**, **Cloudy Marble** and seasonal beers alongside guest beers from independent breweries. Food, including as you might expect vegan meals, is served up to 10 pm from Monday to Friday, until 8 pm on Fridays but only to 4 pm on Saturdays. The splendid polished

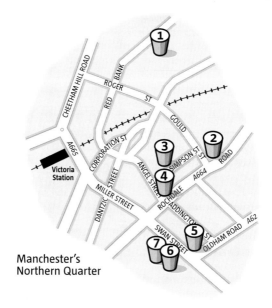

Manchester's
Northern Quarter

granite exterior is complemented by the green and brown
tiling inside. And the floor does slope towards the bar in the
main room – you have not had too many, so far. From the
rear tap room you can view the brewery.

Move on by going back a few yards down Gould Street,
turning left along Durant Street and Simpson Street to
School Street where the **Pot of Beer** (3) is on the corner of
New Mount Street. It's not as complicated as it reads. This
small pub is warm and friendly and a half wall separates
the two rooms. Locally brewed **Boddingtons Bitter** and
Robinson's Dark Mild are served along with up to five guest
beers. It opens all day from noon except Sundays when the
hours are from 1 pm to 7 pm. Polish food is a speciality and
is served on most days until 9 pm.

Turn left on leaving, left again into Ludgate Street and
right into Dyche Street for the **Beer House** (4) on Angel Street.
This is an extremely popular one-bar pub selling **John
Smith's Bitter**, **Taylor Landlord** and an outstanding range of
guest beers, always including a mild, from its 15 hand pulls

as well as German and Belgian beers and two ciders.
There are good value lunches with evening meals on
Thursdays until 8 pm. The upstairs function room is
used for the pub's regular themed beer festivals.

Turn left out of the pub and cross the busy Rochdale
Road and go along the full length of
Addington Street. Turn right into
Oldham Road and right again
into Swan Street for **Bar Fringe** (5).
It is styled as a 'Belgian Brown Bar'
and specialises in Belgian, Dutch
and German beers both draught
and bottled but there are also
four hand pulls serving British
real ales including ones from
the **Bank Top Brewery** in
Bolton, **Boggart Hole Clough**,
a few miles up the road and
other local micros. It opens
all day from noon and food
is served up to 7 pm.

Cross Swan Street for the
final two stops on this crawl.
First comes the **Burton Arms** (6)
a two-roomed pub that also provides accommodation
(0161 834 3455). It opens all day from noon and **Theakston
Cool Cask** and usually a guest ale or two are served. It is
narrow, dark and atmospheric, convivial and well patronised.

Next door but one is the **Smithfield Hotel** (7) (0161 839
4424). This residential hotel provides reasonably-priced
accommodation and a fine selection of beers including a
house beer from **Phoenix** and **Greene King XX Mild** which is
difficult to find even in East Anglia where it hails from.
Up to four guests are also on sale, some by gravity in jugs
straight from the cellar. The pub is open all day from noon and
inexpensive food is served. It is the venue for regular
beer festivals specialising in new micro-breweries from all
over Britain. Continue along Swan Street, across the lights
into Miller Street and Victoria Station is less than half a
mile away.

COMMUTER LAND, the M25, ferries to the continent, the Downs, race courses, pretty market towns, chocolate box villages and oast houses are just a few of the identifying marks of Kent, Surrey and Sussex and a sizeable lump of Greater London. There is so much to see.

Up to the 1950s whole families – thousands of them – used to flock from the east end of London to Kent and Sussex making their home in a bare wooden hut for three weeks to pick hops. Hops – the essential ingredient in beer for flavour and preservation. Nowadays the hop plants are smaller and easier to get at and the job is mainly mechanised. But the region remains England's hop garden and one can expect to find good beer here.

There are 30 thriving breweries in this attractive corner of England and many of their beers can be found on the five pub crawls. In south London a new tramway system allows us to visit a selection of pubs close to its stops; two commuter suburbs, a market town and a seaside town famous for oysters provide the other four.

Carshalton

CARSHALTON HAS BEEN a medieval manor, home to the gentry, an industrial village in the age of water power and finally it was engulfed by inter-war semis. Today the mills are gone and the River Wandle is a quiet backwater rather than a hive of industry, but each phase of Carshalton's history has left its mark, and the centre of the town still has plenty of traces of its rural past. The fact that it was once a place of some importance is reflected in the well-pubbed centre. But gone is one of its finest houses, the King's Arms, which took a direct hit from a wartime flying bomb. Also lost is the Swan, from where the fast carriages used to leave for London in the 18th century. However a good choice remains and, unusually for today, half of them still have separate public bars.

Visitors are advised to arrive by train and start the crawl at Carshalton Station, less than half an hour from Victoria. Alternatives are the 157 bus from Morden underground station which stops at the station, or the 726 bus which runs from Heathrow to Bromley and stops in the High Street.

On leaving the station turn right down to West Street where you bear left, passing the Hope on the left and starting the crawl across the road in the **Race Horse** (1). The emphasis in the saloon bar is on good food, the public bar is comfortable and plain and a good range of beers is available – usually **Courage**, **Gale's** and guest beers from micro-breweries. The present building, not without interest, is early 20th century, and replaced a ramshackle wooden building in what was reckoned to be Carshalton's worst slum, the notorious Race Horse Yard.

Continue up West Street past some handsome houses, the former Swan Inn on the corner of Old Swan Yard, and the unusual water tower of Carshalton House (behind the high wall), turn right at the junction, following the wall to the **Windsor Castle** (2) at the crossroads. Built about 1860,

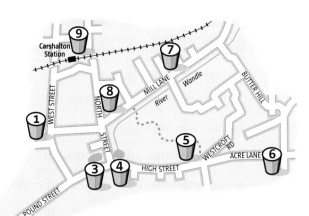

just as Carshalton was beginning to feel the growth of London, this now single-bar pub was badly gutted by fire in 1978 but faithfully reconstructed. It sells **Fuller's London Pride** and up to six guest beers with four-pint jugs for the cost of three and some fine food. It is a former Greater London Pub of the Year and frequent winner of the local CAMRA award.

Retrace your steps back down Pound Street to the **Greyhound** (3), Carshalton's most famous and photogenic old coaching inn overlooking the ponds (020 8647 1511). Architecturally the inn is a happy mixture of two buildings, and they can be seen to advantage from across the ponds, the older part is to the east, weatherboarded, and probably dating back to the late 17th century and the 'modern' addition is from 1840 or so. The name is understood to have been taken from the heraldic arms of the Gaynesfords, an old Carshalton family. Before the pond was divided by a bridge and causeway in 1828 the only way through was via the 'splash' opposite the pub (the two ramps are still quite visible), and the landlord kept a pair of strong horses to rescue hapless travellers who got stuck. This is one of **Young's** flagship hotels and the renovations done in 2001 have retained the quietly civilised atmosphere of the Swan bar at the front of the building with its 250-year-old greyhound mosaic at its threshold that was rediscovered in 1969 and its more mature clientele. In the main building, the large drinking area which surrounds an island bar has several distinctive areas and offers an ambience for most tastes. The pub was named local CAMRA Pub of the Year for 2001–2. There is a full range of **Young's** beers including seasonal ones and guest beers from **Smiles**. The menu is extensive and well praised and accommodation is available in a sensitive new hotel extension at the rear of the building.

Leave the Greyhound and continue on the pleasant footpath overlooking the ponds, skirting the parish churchyard, past the *Woodman Wine Bar* and the **Coach and Horses** (4) at the other corner of the ponds with its nicely tiled exterior and **London Pride**, **Greene King IPA** and sometimes a guest beer on the bar. Carry on up the High Street to the **Fox and Hounds** (5) at the far end. It once had a rambling stream rather than a busy road outside but the building is old, probably early 18th century although it has been considerably altered and opened up inside. A mid-19th century poet in a nearby workhouse gives us a clue as to how the pub got its name:

The Fox and Hounds whither hunters resort,
When they've done a day's murder they call Christian sport.

It can get rather noisy on weekend evenings when it is best avoided unless you are a karaoke fan. It is now a Festival Ale House with ten hand pumps and a beer range that runs from the predictable to the interesting but always changes. Food is available except on Sunday evenings.

If time permits, a detour is recommended at this point along the main road which becomes Acre Lane into Wallington Green which is just a few yards beyond the Carshalton boundary. Here, on the Green is the **Duke's Head** (6) (020 8647 1595) another **Young's** house selling **Bitter**, **Special** and seasonal beers. The exterior of this handsome listed building is early 19th century although the hotel to its right dates back to all of AD 2000! The saloon bar is big with separate areas; the public bar is pleasant enough although rather noisy – but one advantage is that the beer is cheaper in here. The locked door between the two used to be the off-licence, a one-time common feature of many pubs. Retrace your steps to the Fox and Hounds. On the way, across the lights and downhill, you can glimpse the *Rose and Crown*, the former tap of Boorne and Co, a local brewery that closed in 1931.

From the Fox and Hounds, if it is daylight, go through the park (the entrance is down the drive to right of pub car park) turning right at the children's playground and down to the River Wandle, exiting by the gate on to Mill Lane. The **Lord Palmerston** (7) is 100 yards to the right. In the evenings and when it is dark the park gate at the far end may be locked so take Westcroft Road which is the left fork beyond the Fox and Hounds. Go through the sports centre car park, exit at far right-hand corner (cycle route sign), and take the footpath to the right to join Butter Hill. Then bear left past a parade of shops, cross the river, turn left and down Mill Lane for 200 yards to the pub. Mill Lane was once Carshalton's industrial area, first with a series of water mills and more recently with some large chemical factories that have now gone.

This is a handsome building – note the old red Courage sign outside – little altered, and retaining a lively public bar with a collection of chamber pots. It continues to sell **Courage** beers along with **Greene King IPA**. Meals are not served at weekends.

Turn right up Mill Lane to the **Sun** (8), an imposing Victorian railway hotel with impressive decorated brickwork – it is a Grade II listed building. This is another pub that has retained its down-to-earth public bar along with the large and interesting saloon around the corner in North Street. **Fuller's London Pride** and **Greene King Old Speckled Hen** are the regular beers with guests. There is no food at weekends. It is a pub for locals but with a varied clientele from bikers to bridge players and a young crowd at weekends. Legend has it that the pub got its name because the rooms of the hotel received the sun all day from dawn to dusk due to its prominent position on a triangular south-facing plot.

The last stop is just a short walk up North Street, under the railway bridge and on the left. The **Railway Tavern** (9),

built two years after the railway came in 1870, is a modest pub compared to the Sun but makes a pleasant end to the crawl. It lost its public bar in the 1970s but it remains intimate and pleasant with a small beer garden for good weather drinking. Amongst other curiosities this pub has a railway clock that keeps good time and two marbles teams. It is the only **Fuller's** tied house in the town and sells **London Pride** and **ESB**. It is about five minutes' walk back to the station, retracing your steps under the bridge and up the hill.

Croydon tramlink crawl

THIS IS NO ORDINARY PUB CRAWL – Croydon Tramlink is
southern England's first modern tram system, and although
focused on Croydon it reaches out several miles on either
side, to Beckenham and Wimbledon. Our trip takes us from
one end to the other. If you travel from west to east, the tram
takes a slightly different route through Croydon centre and
this will affect your itinerary a little (but see below). The crawl
could easily take up to a whole day to do but you can miss
out some stops or split it into two separate excursions. There
are easy links to the Wimbledon and South Merton crawl
(see *Fifty Great Pub Crawls*) and the Carshalton crawl (qv).

To start the crawl either take a train to Beckenham
Junction (from Victoria, there is a fast and frequent service)
or to East Croydon, and catch the No 2 Beckenham Junction
tram to the terminus.

The first pub is the **Jolly Woodman** (1) in Chancery Lane
about ten minutes' walk from the tram terminus. It is a
pleasant old-fashioned pub with a rural feel in a charming
lane of Victorian cottages. The pub has a pleasant courtyard
garden at the rear. The beers on sale are **Harveys Sussex Best
Bitter**, **Fuller's London Pride**, **Draught Bass** and a house beer
brewed by Bass. There is food at lunchtimes and on
weekdays the pub closes at 2.30 pm for two hours.

Walk back to the tram station and take the next tram as far
as Addiscombe. From there the **Claret Free House** (2) is but a
minute's walk – go back to the road at the end of the platform
and turn left over the tracks. It has a single bar in a conversion
of a former shop – the recreation has left quite an authentic
pub atmosphere with old brewery mirrors and historic
photographs of the area. It is a deservedly regular *Good Beer
Guide* entry, a rare outlet for **Palmer** (Dorset) **IPA**, and offers
other guest beers, usually from smaller breweries, as well
as **Shepherd Neame Spitfire**. It opens all permitted hours and
serves lunches during the week and filled rolls on Saturdays.

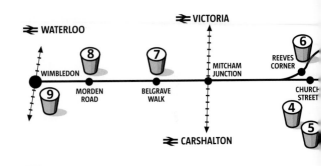

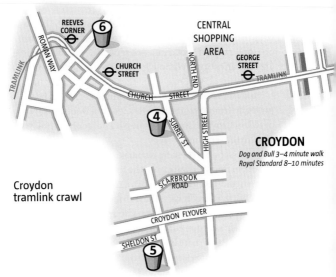

CROYDON

Dog and Bull 3–4 minute walk
Royal Standard 8–10 minutes

Croydon tramlink crawl

Another couple of stops on the tram take us to Lebanon Road, on the outskirts of Croydon. A five-minute walk down Lebanon Road takes us to the **Builders Arms** (3), a **Fuller's** house selling **Chiswick Bitter**, **London Pride**, **ESB** and seasonal beers. It has two interconnected bars that retain their separate characters. The plusher left-hand saloon is a good place to eat at lunchtimes and early evenings. It can get noisy at times but is still worth a visit.

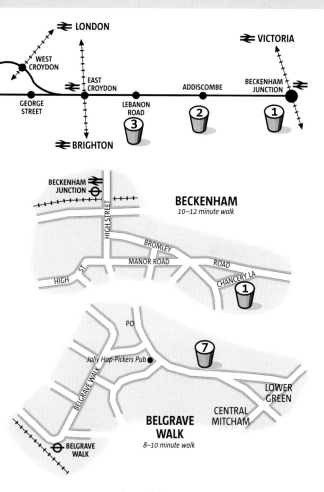

Carry on and get off the tram at George Street, and follow the tracks along for 200 yards before turning left into Surrey Street which hosts a lively street market during the week. Or stay on until the Church Street stop and retrace the tracks for 150 yards for the **Dog and Bull** (4), a former London CAMRA Pub of the Year and one of the highlights of the crawl. There has been a pub on the site since the 15th century. This is a fine building in all ways with a handsome

dark red-brick frontage. This **Young's** house serves **Bitter**,
Special and seasonal beers and there are good value
lunches. It is down-to-earth, basic and lively just as a good
town pub should be. It has been seamlessly extended into a
former shop next door, and has the benefit of an attractive
courtyard garden which is a pleasant option in summer.
Prince Charles visited here when he came to Croydon in
1995, and the photo of him pulling a pint in the pub is on
the walls of many Young's houses. He looks distinctly more
uneasy behind the bar than his grandmother did when she
performed a similar task some time earlier.

If there is time to try another pub then carry on up
Surrey Street to the top and turn right into Scarbrook Road
and left at the bottom. There under the flyover is the **Royal
Standard** (5), a cosy **Fuller's** pub which, like the Dog and Bull,
was once London CAMRA Pub of the Year. The full range of
Fuller's beers is available. And another option is the
Tamworth Arms (6), in Tamworth Road, a **Young's** house with
a single horseshoe bar and just two minutes from Church
Street tram stop.

If you are travelling from the Wimbledon end, the nearest tram stop for the Dog and Bull is Reeves Corner. Alight here and follow the tram tracks straight ahead, as the tram turns off left, go past the George Street stop and then continue as above.

Get back on the No 1 Wimbledon tram and a longer ride takes you through Mitcham to Belgrave Walk, where you will need the map to navigate the modern housing estate and arrive on the main road by the Jolly Hop-Pickers pub where you turn right and 200 yards along on the left is the **Bull** (7), arguably the best of Mitcham's many pubs. It is an early Victorian two-bar **Young's** house with a garden which is still very much a locals' pub without the intrusion of modern distractions – conversation dominates. It sells **Bitter** and **Special**.

Two stops further on is Morden Road where the **Princess of Wales** (8) which featured in the Merton and South Wimbledon crawl in *Fifty Great Pub Crawls* is close by. Turn left and follow the main road north. The building is a handsome mid-Victorian outpost in a messy, modern urban area. This **Young's** pub sells **Bitter**, **Special** and seasonal beers. Food is served every lunchtime and early evenings during the week. There is a single bar but with distinct areas and a patio. It closes Mondays to Thursdays in the afternoons. It used to be called the Prince of Wales and was renamed in 1997 after a refurbishment.

Return to the Morden Road tram stop and ride to the tram terminus at Wimbledon. Turn right on to the main road and just two minutes' walk away is the **Alexandra** (9), a **Young's** house with three distinct drinking areas arranged around a central bar. The pub retains some character, although a big-screen TV may appear when there's a big football match on. There is a roof garden open in the summer.

Dorking

THIS IS ONE OF SURREY'S many pleasant market towns and its parish church spire at 210 feet is one of the tallest in England. It retains an old world charm with many attractive bow-fronted shops. It is well supplied with pubs of all types and several are quite historic. Your crawl starts at Dorking West railway station which is on the cross country line connecting Gatwick with Guildford and Reading.

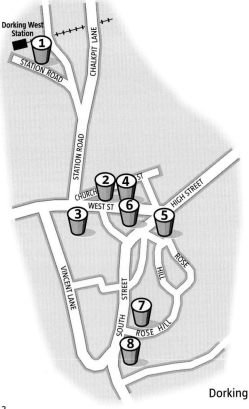

Dorking

The main line station, Dorking North, with trains from London and the south coast is about ten minutes' walk away.

Immediately outside the station is the first stop, the **Pilgrim** (1) in Station Road. It is busy with workers from the nearby industrial estate at lunchtimes but becomes a local in the evenings. The single room sells **Adnams Bitter**, **Fuller's London Pride**, **Ringwood Old Thumper** and occasional guest beers. Food is served except on Sundays. Shove-ha'penny is played in the bar and boules, hop-scotch and badminton in the garden. Beer festivals are held twice a year and there is also frequent outdoor entertainment. Accommodation is available (01306 889951).

Turn left and take about a quarter mile walk down Station Road turning left into West Street and the brick-built **Star Inn** (2) is on your left. This is an attractive pub both outside and in. It is friendly and quite cosy. It sells **Greene King IPA** and a guest beer together with bar snacks and main meals.

Across the road is the **Old House at Home** (3). This 15th-century inn fits well into a street laced with antique shops and is splendidly attired with hanging baskets in summer and there is a pleasant patio garden. The interior is delightfully decorated with brassware and the like. On the hand pulls are **Young's Bitter**, **Special** and **Winter Warmer** in season. Meals are served up to 9 pm except on Sunday evenings. Conversation is important in this pub which unfortunately closes in the afternoons.

Go back across the road and walk 50 yards or so to the **King's Arms** (4). This is one of Dorking's oldest pubs originally built in 1405 as three farm-workers' cottages becoming a

coaching inn in the middle of the 16th century. There is a central bar linked by dining and drinking areas selling **Greene King IPA**, **Wadworth 6X**, **Fuller's London Pride**, **Tetley Bitter**, **Draught Bass** and one or two guest ales usually from one of the smaller independents. An area at the back is a no-smoking bar at lunchtimes and a restaurant at night. The pub opens all day but there is no food on Sundays and Mondays.

Walk to the end of West Street, turn right into South Street and opposite you is the **Bull's Head** (5). This is a lively and well-decorated old coaching inn, part of the Gale's estate. There are lots of photographs of old Dorking on the walls. From the U-shaped bar, parts of which are designated as no-smoking at lunchtimes, **Gale's Butser Bitter** (sold as Bull's Head Bitter), **GB**, **HSB** and **Draught Bass** with either a guest ale or one of Gale's seasonal beers are sold. Lunches are served except on Sundays.

Cross the road for the **Spotted Dog** (6), a comfortable pub with attractive bow windows and a step to catch the unwary. Meals are served except on weekend evenings. On the hand pumps are **Courage Best Bitter**, **Fuller's London Pride** and **Young's Bitter**. There is a large garden with several pet animals and a separate children's play area.

Turn right out of the pub and walk about 200 yards down South Street crossing the road at some stage for the **Cricketers** (7). This well-established **Fuller's** pub is dominated by the single bar with standing room and seats on all sides. The walls are of brick and decorated with sporting pictures particularly of cricket. Outside is a Georgian walled garden. It sells **Chiswick Bitter**, **London Pride**, **ESB** and **Fuller's** seasonal ales and lunches are served except on Sundays. The cellar is built of brick-lined sandstone which keeps the beers at a constant temperature and in excellent condition. This *Good Beer Guide* regular opens all day.

Go a little further on to where the road becomes Horsham Road for the **Queen's Head** (8) which is another **Fuller's** pub serving **Chiswick Bitter**, **London Pride**, **ESB** and the seasonal specials. It is a good looking, family-run, very lively pub and families are welcome in the large garden. It serves lunches but not on Sundays. The walk back to Dorking West is relatively easy.

Kingston upon Thames

THIS IS ONE OF THE GREENEST parts of Greater London with the enormous lungs of Bushy Park, Hampton Court Park, Richmond Park and Wimbledon Common surrounding it. This stretch of the Thames valley is mainly residential and within it there is a selection of fine pubs not too tightly spread and offering everything from simplicity to tradition and elegance and an excellent selection of beers. The crawl extends for about 1½ miles. It features five pubs, well spaced out.

It starts at Kingston railway station which has regular services from central London. Turn left out of the station and then right into Canbury Park Road and the first pub the **Canbury Arms** (1) is at the corner of Elm Road. This Victorian building houses a comfortable and friendly, no-nonsense drinkers' pub run by CAMRA members. On the taps are **Adnams Broadside**, **Courage Best Bitter**, **Greene King Old Speckled Hen**, **Wychwood Hobgoblin** and guest ales as well as a real cider. It is the home to three friendly dogs so take care to shut the 'child' gate behind you when leaving! It was Greater London Pub of the Year in 2000.

Turn right into Elm Road and follow this round for 500 yards to the **Wych Elm** (2), on your left.

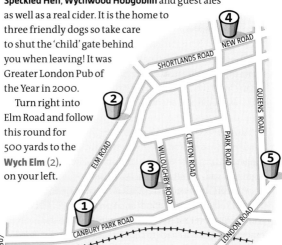

This is a very traditional two-bar pub with a basic public bar and a comfortable and decorative lounge. And at the back is a pleasant garden; the pub has won awards for its floral displays. It is a **Fuller's** house with **Chiswick Bitter**, **London Pride** and **ESB** on sale along with home-cooked lunches from Mondays to Saturdays. It closes in the afternoons except at weekends. The pub is named after a tree that grew nearby but is long since gone.

Moving on, cross the road and bear right down Florence Road and take the path through the council flats. Bear right at the end and the **Willoughby Arms** (3) is on the corner of Willoughby Road and Lowther Road. It is a large two-bar local with a friendly clientele, a house cat and newspapers to read. On the bars are **Fuller's London Pride**, **Taylor Landlord** and guest beers. It has Cask Marque accreditation. There is a strong sports following and it was recently Whitbread Community Pub of the Year and CAMRA's Greater London Pub of the Year in 2001. There are beer festivals on St George's Day and on Hallowe'en. The pub opens all day and managed to retain its 10.30 am opening.

Go back to Elm Road and turn right along Shortlands Road and at the top go into Park Road and cross over into New Road and halfway along is the **Park Tavern** (4) a free house and North Kingston's 'hidden gem'. It sells **Young's Bitter**, **Fuller's London Pride** and three frequently-changing guest beers. It is a genuine free house and an excellent community local attracting a slightly more mature crowd, many of whom are just 'taking the dog for a walk' to nearby Richmond Park. The single bar is decorated with old pictures, clocks and an inventive display of the many pump clips used over the years.

Turn left out of the pub and then right at the top of New Road into Queens Road. Follow it straight along towards Kingston Hill and about 800 yards on the left at the end is your final call, the **Albert Arms** (5) a **Young's** house that was once a hotel and dominates the corner of Kingston Hill. Usually reliable **Young's Bitter** and **Special** are served in a smart, split-level multi-area bar which has recently been renovated. The way back to the station is by London Road, Birkenhead Avenue and Cromwell Road.

Whitstable

WHITSTABLE is situated on the north Kent coast, easily accessible by a direct rail service from London Victoria in an hour and 20 minutes. It is equidistant from its seaside neighbour of Herne Bay and the cathedral city of Canterbury and a reasonable bus service connects the three areas. The town is famous for oysters and it still has a busy working harbour where fresh fish and seafood are for sale. Several excellent restaurants sell local oysters and it is celebrated in a week long festival in July.

This is a compact town that is easily explored on foot. It has a lot of good pubs and this crawl has a selection to give a flavour of the town. The tour is quite short and easily achievable in an afternoon or evening. *Ales and Tales: pubs in the story of Whitstable* is highly recommended. Copies are on sale at the Visitor Information Centre (01227 275482) and the Whitstable Improvement Trust.

Bus arrivals from Canterbury should alight outside the Co-op in Oxford Street and walk back 40 yards towards the railway bridge. From Herne Bay get off at St Alphege School in Oxford Street and continue in the same direction for 130 yards. If travelling by train, turn left out of the railway station, down the slight hill turning left into Railway Avenue. At the mini roundabout, turn left into Cromwell Road and continue to the junction of Oxford Street.

In all three cases you should be at the first stop, the **East Kent** (1). This 200-year-old, imposing building became a pub in 1860 to serve the trade from the new railway line from London – the station was then on the nearby railway bridge. The pub has a central bar and comfortable snug. **Shepherd Neame Master Brew Bitter** and **Spitfire** are on draught along with the company's seasonal beer. No food is available, however, the pub is very near the Shobab, reputedly the best Indian restaurant in town. There is live music on Fridays when the pub can get rather busy.

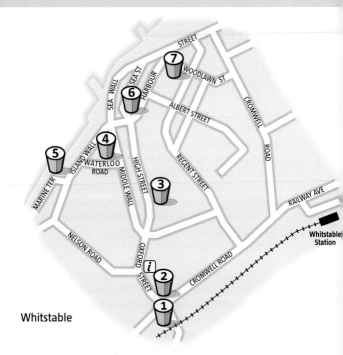

Whitstable

On leaving turn left and continue down Oxford Street and the **Coach and Horses** (2) is about 50 yards on your right, just before the library. This is a cosy pub with low ceilings and a separate snug that dates from the 1830s. **Shepherd Neame Master Brew Bitter** and a seasonal beer are on the hand pumps. It serves good value home-cooked meals and has a small restaurant area. There is a sun-trapped rear patio.

Turn right and carry on down Oxford Street (which becomes High Street) for 200 yards and the *Good Beer Guide* listed **Ship Centurion** (3) is on your right. This is a busy town-centre pub festooned with hanging baskets in summer. Comfortable high-backed bar-stools surround the bar where **Adnams Bitter**, **Elgood's Black Dog Mild** (the only mild in town) and two guest beers are always available. The guest beers change frequently and the pub offers the best beer range in town. Home-cooked bar snacks are served all day until 9 pm including some authentic German dishes –

on Saturdays schnitzels are the only thing served.
Fascinating photographs of old Whitstable, complete with
potted histories, hang in the clean and tidy public bar.
Entertainment includes live music on Thursday evenings
and Sunday afternoons. The pub opens all day.

From here turn right and at St Alphege's Church cross
the High Street and go down Kemp Alley which is alongside
the Whitstable Playhouse. At the junction with Middle
Wall, turn right and continue for 200 yards, past the public
car park and the **Smack** (4) is on your left. The pub is named
after a type of oyster barge. This is a traditional, and often
quiet, small pub with a central bar and a real fire but
limited seating. **Shepherd Neame Master Brew Bitter** and
occasionally **Spitfire** are on draught. Pub food is available.
It has the best pub loos in town – ladies, check out the
selection of toiletries! There is live music on Sunday nights.

On leaving turn right and then right again into Waterloo
Road. Continue for 125 yards to its junction with Island Wall
and turn left. After 100 yards turn right into Marine Gap
alley – opposite 57 Island Wall – and the **Old Neptune** (5)
is at the end of the alleyway on the beach.

This white weatherboarded pub
has the best location in town –
right on the seashore with
plenty of tables outside
there's no finer place to be
on a sunny day.
It attracts lots
of visitors,
particularly
families.

Fuller's London Pride and
Flowers Original are on sale, but drinks taken outside have
to be served in plastic glasses. Food is normally available.
The original building was badly damaged in the great
storm of 1853 and completely swept away in 1898. It was
rebuilt then and has since survived further storms.

Go back down Marine Gap alleyway and turn left into
Island Wall. Continue 300 yards along and you are now in
Terry's Lane. At the junction turn left into Horsebridge

Road and the **Prince Albert** (6) is 40 yards on in Sea Street. This pub is near the beach and the very popular Royal Naval Oyster Stores restaurant. It has one, small bar with old Tomson and Wootton Brewery windows and a mark from the 1953 floods on the wall. This *Good Beer Guide* pub has three beers on tap – usually **Fuller's London Pride**, **Greene King IPA** and **Marston's Pedigree** – although a guest beer sometimes replaces one of these. Good value, home-cooked food – including steak and oyster pie – is served daily at lunchtimes and from 6 until 8 pm. There is also a small patio with a couple of tables.

Turn left from here and go down Red Lion Lane past the taxi office. Turn left into Harbour Street and continue as far as the Quayside pub then turn right into Woodlawn Street and the **New Inn** (7) is on your right. This small, friendly back-street local was built in the 19th century to serve local oyster dredgers, mariners and shipyard craftsmen. It is still very much a community pub and supports active darts and quiz teams and charity events. Etched glass in the doors defines the original four rooms into which this long, narrow pub was once divided. A sympathetic extension provides a games area. This long-standing *Good Beer Guide* entry serves **Shepherd Neame Master Brew Bitter** at the best price in Whitstable. No food is served but a complimentary seafood selection is on the bar on Sunday lunchtimes.

For a bus to Canterbury retrace your steps to Harbour Street and at the Quayside pub, turn left and the bus stop is 75 yards on, opposite VC Jones fish and chip shop. Allow three minutes from the New Inn. To Herne Bay go the same way but turn right at the Quayside pub, then cross the road at the zebra crossing opposite the Harbour. Turn right and the bus stop is 300 yards ahead. Allow five minutes.

For the railway station turn right into Woodlawn Street and continue for 170 yards, then at the junction with Cromwell Road turn right by the post box and walk 400 yards up this residential road. Turn left at the mini roundabout into Railway Avenue and the station is 75 yards away on your right. Trains for Thanet depart from this side so cross the bridge if you are going towards London. This walk takes about ten minutes.

THIS IS one of the smallest of the British Tourist Authority's regions. It includes a long reach of the Thames, the Chilterns, a coastal stretch from Portsmouth to Poole and the Isle of Wight.

This is naval and military territory and many service and ex-service men and women will have spent some time in the area. Their memories may be of drinking in pleasant village and street-corner pubs or of the horrors of square-bashing, or even of both. And there are stately homes here, it's where the royals live, some of the world's finest race horses are trained here and millionaires play golf. It is also full of history and is great walking country. There are many great breweries producing prize-winning ales and the home of many clder makers.

Good pubs abound and the two crawls featured are both unusual. One captures the spirit of the ancient pastime of Morris Dance, the other takes a train ride from one seaside resort to another with a couple of stops on the way.

Bampton

The heartland of Morris Dance

BAMPTON – more properly known as Bampton-on-the-Bush – is an ancient Oxfordshire market town and one of the natural homes of Morris Dance – it is claimed that the town has the longest unbroken record for performance. There are currently three sides of dancers in Bampton and they all perform on the traditional day, Spring Bank Holiday Monday; originally on Whit Monday. On this day the Bampton sides can be seen dancing in the streets, yards, gardens and squares of this attractive Cotswold town.

The dancing starts at 8 am and moves through the town at 25 locations until 7 pm when it continues in the streets. The pubs support the local sides and as they are grouped together around the centre of the town it makes a pub crawl at this time a most enjoyable and entertaining one – traditional entertainment and good beer. Bampton can be easily reached by bus from Oxford city centre and Witney.

Morris dancing dates back to the 15th century but it has had many declines and resurgences over the centuries until 1900 from when it has become more popular than ever and today more than 80 sides enjoy the activity as do the spectators. Traditional Cotswold Morris is normally a male activity but there are variations in other parts of England with women's and even mixed sides.

This is a short pub crawl, there being only four pubs in the town – at one time there were 13. However, it does allow you to spend longer in each pub enjoying the good beer. It begins at the eastern edge of the town in the High Street at the **Morris Clown** (1) a former Courage-owned local, with a single L-shaped bar, that was saved from closure many years ago by the present landlord and his father and is now run as a free house. A huge log fire warms the bar, and the walls are decorated with curious murals depicting local people. Aunt Sally, darts and bar billiards are all played in local leagues. Regular beers include **Archers Village**, **Courage Best**

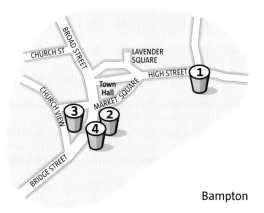

Bampton

Bitter and a number of guest beers as well as a traditional cider. It opens from 5 pm during the week and all day at weekends.

Proceed into the town centre along the High Street for about 200 yards to the Market Square, passing the War Memorial on your way. This commemorates the 51 men of Bampton who lost their lives (and the 40 who were wounded) in the First World War. Out of a total population of 1,300, Bampton sent the remarkable total of more than 250 young men to the war. On the edge of the square is the town hall designed by George Wilkinson of Witney in the 1830s. He was the elder brother of the rather better known William Wilkinson whose designs were used for the Randolph Hotel in Oxford and many other buildings in and around Oxford.

On the corner of the square by the roundabout, you will find the **Talbot Hotel** (2) on the left-hand side of Bridge Street. This is a quiet pub in a very old building with a large lounge bar area with exposed beams and a separate games room. Regular beers include **Fuller's London Pride** and **Hook Norton Best Bitter** and occasional guests often from local micro-breweries.

A short walk of about 40 yards along Bridge Street, and across the road, you will come to the **Horseshoe** (3). This Greene King pub has a light, airy and brightly decorated public bar and a separate lounge bar. Regular beers in this very friendly pub include **Greene King IPA** and **Ruddles County** and seasonal specials. There is often traditional folk music at the weekends.

Go back across the road and next to the Talbot is the last stop at the **Romany Inn** (4). This 17th-century building has in its time served as a temperance hall, a shop and a café. The interior is large but cosy, with three separate areas. It has beamed ceilings, stone walls and a large fireplace. There is also a pleasant beer garden and a children's play area.

An excellent selection of good hot and cold food is on offer in the bar and the restaurant which is no-smoking. The three-course Sunday lunch is highly recommended. Regular beers include **Archers Village** and normally three changing guest beers. On the occasion of the 2003 Spring Bank Holiday Morris Dance festivities the guest list read like a mini beer festival with around 12 beers from all over Britain and a traditional cider. Bed and breakfast accommodation is available (01993 850237).

Poole by train

POOLE is often regarded as Bournemouth's older but less affluent neighbour. No view is passed here on that subject but what can be said with certainty is that in terms of good pubs and good ale Poole stands easily on top. Although it is difficult to identify the boundary between the two towns, Poole is fiercely independent and has great history displayed in its maritime and local history museums and Poole Pottery. The almost land-locked harbour is one of the largest natural harbours in the world.

Because many main line trains from London and Birmingham stop at Bournemouth it is suggested that the crawl starts there or the adjoining Travel Interchange and head west through the suburbs of Poole. The pubs on the crawl are all quite close to the railway stations that are called at. Trains run every half hour and buses (services 101/105) every ten minutes to Branksome Station.

Across Poole Road is the **Branksome Railway Hotel** (1) a late Victorian residential hotel (01202 769555) with two bars connected by an arch. Real ale is only available in the comfortable lounge with its large fireplace and pictures of bygone Poole. On sale are **Fuller's London Pride** and **Hampshire Strong's Best Bitter** along with guest ales from **Hop Back** and **Cottage** breweries and in addition to bar snacks there is an excellent restaurant. The bar is open all day.

Take either the train to Parkstone or bus service 101/103 (every 20 minutes) to Ashley Cross. From the station walk along Station Road into Commercial Road where the bus stop is. All three pubs on this section of the crawl are within a stone's throw.

The first visit is to the **Central Hotel** (2) a mid-Victorian pub that has been in the Hall & Woodhouse estate for more than a century. The hand pumps are on an elaborate and handsome counter in the front bar that also features high ceilings and etched glass windows. On sale are **Badger Best**

Poole by train

and **Tanglefoot** along with seasonal beers including **King &
Barnes Festive** and **Badger Golden Champion**. It opens all day
at weekends but only the side bar (Bar One) is open during
weekday lunchtimes. This is a great music venue upstairs
with an emphasis on blues.

Go a few yards up Parr Street for the **Bermuda Triangle** (3)
a regular *Good Beer Guide* entry with an excellent selection
of real ales on its four hand pulls which change regularly.
One small bar serves several separate drinking areas.
Lunches are served from Mondays to Saturdays. It is full of
Bermuda Triangle memorabilia – maps and newspaper
cuttings – and includes a section of an aircraft's wing
suspended from the ceiling. The pub closes in the
afternoons except at weekends.

Across the road is the **Bricklayers Arms** (4) an upmarket
one-roomed free house with an L-shaped layout. A real fire
with armchairs and a sofa give this pub a homely and
comfortable feeling. Indoor greenery provides a breath of

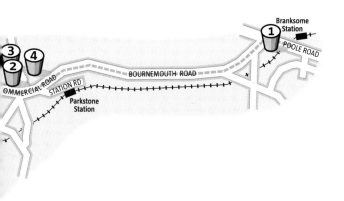

fresh air but the real thing is available in the secluded rear garden or tables at the front. On the hand pulls are **Greene King Abbot**, **Hop Back Summer Lightning** and **Ringwood Best Bitter** and **Fortyniner**. The pub closes in the afternoons.

Take the bus or the train to Poole railway station. Go through the Dolphin shopping centre and down the pedestrianised High Street and on the right is the **Brewhouse** (5). This was formerly the home of Poole Brewery. The brewery has closed and the pub has been sold to **Milk Street Brewery**. A single bar serves a split-level room and tables in the precinct. Despite canned music, conversation reigns in this very friendly pub.

From the precinct turn right into New Orchard and then half right for Market Close and the **Blue Boar** (6). This is a former merchant's house dating from 1750. There is a comfortable and stylish lounge bar and an atmospheric cellar bar where the local folk club meets on Wednesdays and there is more live music on Fridays and Sundays. The pub opens at 5.30 am on May Day when Morris dancers welcome the dawn! Both bars have a nautical theme. The pub sells **Cottage Southern Bitter**, **Courage Best Bitter** and **Directors** and two guest ales and serves lunches. It closes in the afternoons.

Retrace your steps along New Orchard into Old Orchard and turn right on to The Quay for the **Poole Arms** (7) easily spotted by its green tiled front. The roundel high on its fascia is from the Marston's brewery which has no connection with the one in Burton-upon-Trent but was based in Poole until taken over and ceased brewing in 1926. It is probably the best pub along the whole of Poole Quay and is an oasis of calm amongst noisy places aimed at 'yoof'. There is a single flagstone-floored room and an outside drinking area – children are not allowed in the bar. The hand pulls serve **Flowers IPA**, **Hampshire Strong's Best Bitter** and **Ringwood Best Bitter**. Lunches are served in summer. The pub opens all day every day.

The return walk is through the precinct and the shopping centre to the railway station.

Westward Ho!

THE SUNNY SOUTH WEST, England's Riviera, the west country, are just some of the many descriptions England's five westernmost counties attract in tourist literature particularly that of the former Great Western Railway company. It opened up the region for holiday makers and the main line stretches to Penzance, a mere ten miles from Land's End.

With two national parks – Dartmoor and Exmoor – this region has so much to offer the visitor. Some of the most dramatic coastal scenery in the British Isles contrasts with stark moorlands and the beautiful hill country of the Mendips and the Quantocks. Fine old churches and ancient monuments cover the area.

There are great artistic and literary traditions. St Ives is an outpost of the Tate Gallery and the home of many artists; Daphne du Maurier based her most famous novels here, Charles Kingsley's *Westward Ho!* led to the naming of that Devon resort and Thomas Hardy was born, lived, worked and wrote about the area. In *The Trumpet Major* he described the local ale as 'brisk as a volcano, full in body, luminous as an autumn sunset.'

In the three pub crawls along the south coast between Topsham and Penwith you will find some excellent inns and pubs and if you come across beers that fit Hardy's description – then enjoy them.

Around Plymouth's eastern reaches

PLYMOUTH is the supreme naval town with a historical attachment to the sea that dates from before the Domesday Book of 1086. In the 16th century it was the home port of many famous Elizabethan adventurers: Raleigh, Frobisher and Hawkins, and the English fleet under Drake sailed from there to attack the Spanish Armada in 1588. The Hoe (the southern waterfront) is dominated by the Royal Citadel, built by Charles II to replace a Tudor castle. In 1620 the Mayflower with the Pilgrim Fathers sailed for the new world; and in 1690 William III ordered the draining of the marshes to build the Royal Dockyard on the eastern bank of the Tamar. Captain James Cook started his round-the-world exploration from Plymouth in 1772 and two centuries later Sir Francis Chichester completed his circumnavigation of the world here. Following severe bombing in the Second World War it has been rebuilt as a handsome city and there is much to see here – not least some fine pubs.

This pub crawl is along the coast that helps to make up the city's waterfront and it follows part of the route of the South West coastal path. The best way to start the crawl if you are in Plymouth is to catch the No 7 or 7A bus from Royal Parade in the city centre, and ask for Hooe Lake (it is pronounced 'who').

From the bus stop you will see an expanse of grass and to the right and at the far end is the **Royal Oak** (1). It was built, according to a plaque high on its front, 'circa 1887'. It has a brick lower storey and a decorated gothic first floor. The one large bar has maritime memorabilia and local historic photographs. **Young's Special**, **Courage Best Bitter** and **Draught Bass** are on the hand pumps. The bar food is good with occasional theme evenings as well as a range of sandwiches at lunchtimes and in the evenings. A spacious beer garden has uninterrupted views over Hooe Lake,

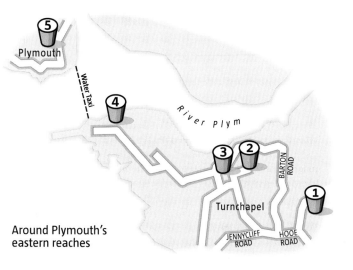

Around Plymouth's eastern reaches

a tidal inlet of the River Plym. Accommodation is available (01752 512900).

After leaving the pub turn right and follow the path beside the sea wall to the road on the far side. Turn right again and take the road alongside the river. Continue past the remains of a bridge and follow the road to the right passing the main gate of the Royal Marine landing craft base. A large gate blocks the way but a wicket gate allows you access to the village of Turnchapel.

Walk along the main street, and where the road splits keep to the left of the railings and on the left amidst the large terraced houses is the **Boringdon Arms** (2) named after the local titled family. The bar is situated on the left and there is a quieter lounge on the right. The range of beers available here is good with **Butcombe Bitter**, **RCH Pitchfork**, **Summerskills Best Bitter**, **Sutton XSB** and a minimum of three guest ales at any time and a traditional cider. There is a beer festival on the last weekend of every odd month – it starts on Friday lunchtime and lasts until the beer runs out. There is music on Wednesdays, Thursdays and Saturdays. The home-made pies are legendary and other freshly-prepared bar meals are available. It opens all day every day. Bed and breakfast is available (01752 402053). The pub has won many CAMRA awards.

On leaving turn left, go down the stone steps, turn left again and walk about 50 yards and on the corner of the crossroads is the **New Inn** (3). It was originally three buildings – a butcher's, a bakery and a tavern but now it provides fine beer, good food and quiet accommodation (01752 402765). The beers available are **Draught Bass**, **Princetown Jail Ale**, **Taylor Landlord**, **Sharp's Doom Bar Bitter** and a good choice of guest beers. The pub is large and several traditional games are played.

After leaving the New Inn turn right to the crossroads and then right again up the steep hill that leads out of the village. Near to the top you can spot a blue plaque on a wall after the village shop which marks the one-time residence of T E Lawrence (Lawrence of Arabia) under his adopted name of Shaw when he served as an Aircraftsman at RAF Mountbatten during the 1920s.

Continue to the top of the hill where you will see, on the right, a signpost directing you along the South West coastal path for Clovelly Bay. Go down the steps to the Marina and at the bottom turn left along the sea wall then follow the road to the left of the red lighthouse as far as the roundabout. From here turn right past the large sheds on your right and take in the fabulous views into Cornwall across Plymouth Sound.

This road leads to the Mountbatten Hotel and its associated **Mountbatten Pub** (4) to the left. This is a modern, purpose-built hotel bar which is large and airy with good views across the River Plym and Plymouth Sound to the Barbican, the Hoe and the Royal Citadel. It has a varied menu of bar food and an ever-changing selection of guest ales, often from local breweries, on the hand pumps. There is a large outside seating area and children are welcome in the pub. It opens all day. Accommodation is available in the hotel (01752 405500).

Outside the Mountbatten there are stunning views across Plymouth Sound and a jetty, which projects into the Sound for 300 yards, is much in use for fishing.

There is a castle dating from the Civil War which can be visited although you have to climb the steep hill that formed part of its defences. A large aircraft propeller stands alongside the car park as a marker to RAF Mountbatten which was located here until the early 1990s.

From here there is a choice of ways back to the city centre. Directly outside the Mountbatten Hotel is a bus terminus with a service to Royal Parade, but the quickest and most pleasant route is to take the water taxi service to the Barbican, a journey of 15 minutes. It runs in the summer up to 11 pm.

Once in the Barbican there is a large range of pubs and restaurants in what is a very small area; but the only pub worthy of note is the **Dolphin** (5) which is kept in the old style with a marble floor. It is the only unspoilt pub in Plymouth's historic centre and **Draught Bass** is drawn straight from barrels on racks behind the bar. This pub, its landlord and its customers have often been subjects for artists including Beryl Cook. The pub windows remember the former Octagon Brewery in the city where brewing ceased in 1970.

Topsham

TOPSHAM remains a village but these days is almost caught up in the Exeter sprawl. It is very popular with the sailing fraternity. However there are historic reminders of its days as a port with riverside warehouses and merchants' houses in the Dutch style. Whichever way you travel to Topsham, start the crawl at the railway station where the bus also stops and a free car park is just 250 yards away.

A gentle stroll of a quarter of a mile along Elm Grove Road on the road to Exmouth away from the station takes you down Bridge Hill to the well-known **Bridge Inn** (1) a must for ale buffs and connoisseurs of good ale with eight to ten beers all drawn on gravity direct from the cellar. They may include **Adnams Broadside**, **Blackawton Westcountry Gold**, **Branscombe Vale Branoc**, **Exe Valley Exeter Old Bitter**, **Otter Ale** and guest beers. It offers friendly service, simple, tasty bar food, no noisy music or machines – just a chatty, relaxed atmosphere and, in winter, a log fire. There are riverside picnic-sets overlooking the weir.

Retrace your steps, back to the station and then along Holman Way towards the Quay to bring you to the **Lighter Inn** (2). This old stone-built former custom house sells three **Badger** beers including **Tanglefoot**, **Best** and a seasonal one. The food here is well recommended and good value. It is a spacious and comfortably refurbished pub with panelling and tall windows looking out over tidal flats, a more intimate side room and tables out on the old quay. There is good value accommodation (01392 875439).

Walk along the lower route on the water's edge to the **Passage House Inn** (3), a lovely old riverside pub with a beer garden but with a major emphasis on food. There are two bistro areas one of which is no-smoking. The draught ales include **Draught Bass**, **Boddingtons Bitter**, **Flowers IPA** and **Wadworth 6X**.

Topsham

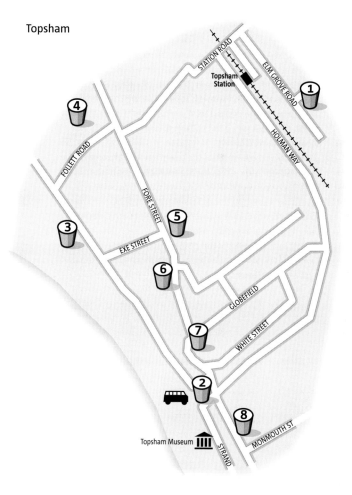

Go up Exe Street and into Fore Street. Turn left towards Exeter and a little way along is the attractive looking *Lord Nelson* (4) but be warned, it does not serve drinks without food. Opposite the top of Exe Street is *Drakes Inn Wine and Ale House* (5) a Heavitree pub that sells only one cask ale.

Alternatively, you could turn right out of Exe Street and down Fore Street is the **Salutation** (6), owned by Punch Taverns and offering two ales from their range. And further down on the left is the **Globe Hotel** (7) a free house dating from the 16th century with an old timbered and panelled bar with a log fire. It offers **Draught Bass**, **Courage Best Bitter** and **Hancock's HB** and sometimes a guest ale. There is good, interesting home-cooked food at reasonable prices. It opens all day and provides good value bed and breakfast accommodation.

Finally at the bottom of the town, having returned to the Lighter, right opposite is the **Steam Packet** (8) another Heavitree house on a boat-builders' quay. It provides several well-kept, varying ales and reasonably-priced bar food. There are dark flagstones, scrubbed boards, wood panelling and stripped masonry.

Beside the Lighter is the bus terminus to travel back to Exeter or you can wander back up Holman Way to the car park or the railway station.

The Bridge Inn, Topsham

THE BRIDGE is one of the least altered pubs in the country –
one not to miss. The attractive pink painted building consists
of two distinct parts: a range dating back to the 18th century
parallel to the road and a later block nearer the river. At the
back there is also a large wing that served as a malt house
when the pub had its own brewery in the 19th century.

It has been in the hands of the same family for more
than a century and its moment of glory came in 1998 when
the Queen paid her only ever official visit to a pub and
accepted a bottle of specially-brewed beer.

What makes the pub so special is the survival of its
separate rooms complete with fittings that must be well
over 100 years old. The spine of the Bridge is a panelled
corridor running parallel with the road. Two rooms open
off to the front, including the tap room with more panelled
walls and fixed seating. Opposite is the servery where up to
ten real ales are served direct from the cask and brought
from the cellar, which involves walking up and down
three steps each time. The servery is known as the 'inner
sanctum' and drinkers can sit there by invitation only.

The most wonderful room is the lounge which is
partitioned from the corridor by a settle that bulges out
into it. There is a log fire in winter. Another delightful
place is the brick-arched
passage between the cellar
and the old malt house.
It contains a furnace
associated with the
old brewery.

137

West Cornwall by bus

THE MOST WESTERLY PUB CRAWL in England is around Cornwall's west Penwith peninsula. It is also one of the most delightful and scenic and, as much of it is done by bus, one of the most relaxing. It starts at Penzance bus station next to the last railway station in England. It uses the No 10 or 10A bus run by First Western National between Penzance and St Just. After Newbridge the 10 goes direct to St Just and the 10A goes around a loop of villages. Services run every half hour through the day, reducing to hourly in the evening. The last bus back to Penzance leaves St Just as late as 11.25 pm so there is plenty of scope for an evening crawl. On Sundays the service is limited to two-hourly and is daytime only. A suggested timetable is given but there is enough flexibility to have many variations as the fancy takes you.

Leave Penzance on the 11.45 am No 10 service which arrives in the quiet hamlet of Newbridge at 12.01 pm just a minute after opening time at the **Fountain Inn** (1). This excellent old granite-built community pub is worth staying at for an hour or so and maybe having lunch. There is a real fire in an enormous granite fireplace, tables made out of disused casks and families and dogs are welcome.

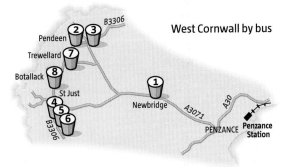

West Cornwall by bus

It sells a full range of **St Austell** beers including seasonal specials and two of them – **Tinners** and **HSD** – are occasionally dispensed by gravity. Wine glass samples of each beer allow you to try before you buy.

The 10A bus leaves Newbridge at 1.31 pm for the eight-minute journey to Pendeen and the **Radjel Inn** (2). This is another comfortable village pub with an interesting history and a splendid pub sign. A radjel is a pile of stones where a fox lives and, while this is clear from the sign, the pub takes its title from the nickname of a former landlord. **St Austell** beers are on sale. The locals play euchre here – a complicated card game that remains very popular in the west country. Accommodation is available (01736 788446).

No more than 200 yards away – two minutes' walk – is the **North Inn** (3), another **St Austell** pub and the third Cask Marque holder on this crawl. This welcoming pub has many photographs and artefacts of the former tin mining industry – the nearby Geevor mine was the last to close in the area and is now a mining museum. Four of the local beers are on sale with occasional variations. The inn is in good walking country, close to the coastal path and in an area of outstanding natural beauty. You can stay here too (01736 788417). Both this and the Radjel open all day.

A suitable bus leaves the North Inn at 2.45 pm for St Just passing the Trewellard and the Queen's Arms which both close at lunchtimes but which the crawl returns to later.

There are five pubs to choose from here but time constraints will limit you to two or three at the most. The **Miners Arms** (4) is recommended; it is a basic local watering-hole just off the village centre, but convivial and welcoming. And there is a change of beer – just the one – but often from the **Skinner's** brewery in Truro. It opens all day.

The **King's Arms** (5) in the Market Square is a fine old granite pub that caters for locals and visitors. It sells **St Austell** beers including one specially brewed for the town festival in July called **Lafrowda Gold**. Food is available lunchtimes and evenings and the pub opens all day.

A pub not to be missed is the magnificent **Star Inn** (6) in Fore Street. Its external appearance belies its superb interior. It is the oldest inn in St Just and the story goes that

John Wesley had lodgings here. It is atmospheric and full of memories of the tin mining industry. The bar is beamed, slate-floored and the centre of the local folk music scene with singalongs on most evenings. **St Austell** beers are served by hand pull and by gravity from wooden casks and traditional cider is also sold. Food is available at lunchtimes and there is also bed and breakfast (01736 788767). There is a beautiful beer garden at the back.

We now backtrack by catching the 5.10 pm bus to the **Trewellard Arms Hotel** (7) in the eponymous village. The journey takes eight minutes. **Sharp's Doom Bar Bitter** and **Eden Ale** are sold. This is a modernised hotel and, slightly bizarrely, doubles as a fish and chip shop reflecting the former occupation of the licensee. Food is available on weekdays in summer and all the year round in the evenings, which can be an attraction in itself for the hungry.

There is a bus at 5.50 pm back towards St Just as far as Botallack for the final stop at the **Queen's Arms** (8). It is only a three-minute trip or it could be walked in about 15 to 20 minutes. The pub opens at 6.30 pm on weekdays and all day at the weekends – so you may have to wait a few minutes for it to open. This pleasant village local is granite-built with beams and although there is only one bar there are several distinct drinking areas. There is a collection of pictures of the mining industry on the walls. It sells **Draught Bass** and two ever-changing local ales that are likely to include some from **Sharp's** and **Skinner's**.

On this timed crawl the return service to Penzance is at 6.53 pm from the Queen's arriving back at 7.22 pm. After this the buses ease out to an hourly service.

Ring the changes if you wish and shorten or alter the crawl to suit you. The pubs around Pendeen are within walking distance of each other but don't walk in the dark as the roads are essentially rural, fairly busy, and have no pavements west of Trewellard.

Casterbridge Ale

IT WAS OF THE MOST beautiful colour that
the eye of an artist in beer could desire;
full in body, yet brisk as a volcano; piquant,
yet without a twang; luminous as an autumn
sunset; free from streakiness of taste; but,
finally, rather heady. The masses worshipped
it, the minor gentry loved it more than wine,
and by the most illustrious county families
it was not despised. Anybody brought up for
being drunk and disorderly in the streets of
its natal borough, had only to prove that he
was a stranger to the place and its liquor to
be honourably dismissed by the magistrates,
as one overtaken in a fault that no man could
guard against who entered the town unawares.

From *The Trumpet Major*, Thomas Hardy

God's own country

SOME FOLK CALL IT God's Own Country. Others, less respectful, say that Yorkshiremen are merely Scots without the generous streak or Lancastrians without the sophistication. But, whatever the view, there can be no doubt that it is a much visited county for whatever reason, be it the scenery, history, culture, architecture or sport. And visitors are made truly welcome – ask the folk who know best, the ones who live there.

And no one would deny that there are some good pubs in Yorkshire. Again ask those that know best. CAMRA has chosen a Yorkshire venue for its annual meeting on six occasions in the last 30 years and everyone knows that such a weekend is as much a social event as a business meeting. There are some right good ale houses in the county of the broad acres and they charge decent prices. They have to, because Yorkshire folk drink in them.

The crawls detailed in this section cover a variety of towns and it includes one that uses public transport and another that is a brewery crawl as well as a pub crawl. They offer you a good excuse to visit Yorkshire for a few days and complete the handful of crawls. As if you needed an excuse.

Addingham

ADDINGHAM is one of the lesser-known treasures of
Wharfedale because for many years it suffered from severe
traffic pollution. Since the building of a bypass it is regaining
its inheritance and is a delightful place to visit with some
splendid Yorkshire stone houses on the main street,
picturesque gardens, an interesting 15th-century church,
five unspoilt and traditional pubs and the usual village
amenities. The pubs are well spread out in this mile-long
straggling village and make an excellent pub crawl with a
good choice of beers, first-rate food and some interesting
historical notes. Halfway down the main street is a
well-drawn plan of Addingham full of detail and interest.

Buses (service 784 and X84) run from Leeds, Otley and
Ilkley through Addingham to Skipton and back, hourly for
most of the day including Sundays, and there are five stops
in the village. The best stop from either direction is at the
top of the village at the Craven Heifer; it is then an easy
downhill walk to the other pubs and there is a bus stop by
the Fleece. All the pubs have car parks and outdoor
drinking areas.

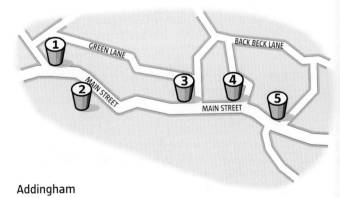

Addingham

The **Craven Heifer** (1) (01943 830106) sells **Tetley Mild** and **Bitter**, **Black Sheep Best Bitter** and **Special**. It was built in 1820 on the site of a previous pub dating from 1687. The name comes from a gigantic beast born in 1807 and reared at Gargrave by Reverend William Carr incumbent at Bolton. Its height at the shoulder was 5′ 2″ and length nose to rump 11′ 2″. It weighed 176 stones 4 lbs. Up to 1817 a picture of it was on notes of the Craven Bank. Several pubs including at least ten in Yorkshire have been named after it and a drawing of the heifer is in the bar. An L-shaped bar serves a large main room and a restaurant where good quality food is served including interesting dishes such as Louisiana Catfish with wild rice. The pub closes in the afternoon except on Sundays when it opens all day with meals into the early evening.

Walk downhill and cross the road to the **Sailor** (2) (01943 830216) which was once called the Jolly Sailor and is said to have been a mariners recruitment office despite being 70 miles from the sea! It is more than 200 years old although it was largely rebuilt in 1838. It sells **Tetley Bitter**, **Black Sheep Best Bitter** and **Marston's Pedigree**. The bar serves a large, comfortable front room and to the left are two pleasant dining rooms where good value meals are served at lunchtimes and evenings until 9.30 pm. There is a most attractive suntrap of a garden at the back of the pub.

Cross the road and at the **Swan Inn** (3) (01943 830375) the beers on sale are **Tetley Bitter**, **Greene King Abbot**, **Everards Tiger** and a guest ale. It was probably built about 1820 but its origins are in the 16th century. At the rear is the now derelict one-time village mortuary and chapel of rest. The pub has four rooms including a tiny snug, real fires, flagged floors, a lot of cricket memorabilia and all the character of a turn of the century inn. The pub food and sandwiches are good and reasonably priced. It is open all day except during weekday afternoons in winter.

Further down Main Street is the **Crown Inn** (4) (01943 830274) where **Theakston Best Bitter** and **Tetley Bitter** are on sale. This pub was built in 1769 as the datestone above the main door indicates and at one time had a brewery behind it. There is a large main room containing the bar with two small rooms of great character opening off. There are flagged floors and open fires and a fine brass collection. It is open all day and although it is very much a locals' pub all are made welcome.

The last stop is at the **Fleece** (5) (01943 830491) that has **Tetley Mild**, **Bitter** and **Burton Ale** on the pumps. It was built in 1740 on the site of what was then the village's oldest pub which dated from before 1600. It is a bustling, friendly pub where good value food is served in the bars and the restaurant both at lunchtimes and in the evenings. There is jazz on Wednesdays with the generous offer of a free supper besides, and folk music on Sundays.

Beverley

BEVERLEY, the county town of the East Riding of Yorkshire, lies ten miles north of Hull, with regular bus and rail links connecting the two. The prosperous market town has a charter dating from 1129, it flourished on the wool trade in the Middle Ages, which saw the construction of the stunning Gothic Minster. It is an attractive town in which many Georgian townhouses survive. The extensive Westwood pastures off the York road are an attraction for walkers.

The crawl starts at the bus station by crossing New Walkergate at the traffic lights to reach the **Cornerhouse** (1), a well-respected pub and café-bar. It has recently been transformed from a Firkin identikit pub but before that, for most of its life, this historic building was a two-roomed Tetley boozer known as the Valiant Soldier. Regular beers still include **Tetley Bitter** along with **Taylor Landlord**, **Greene King Abbot**, **Rooster's Yankee** and several guest beers. Around 50 single malt whiskies and **Weston's Old Rosie cider** are on offer. Food is rather special, mostly home made with vegetarian and vegan choices. A full English breakfast is served at weekends from 10 am.

Turn left on leaving the Cornerhouse and cross New Walkergate to reach Beverley's most famous pub situated in Hengate, and back to back with the bus station, the **White Horse Inn** (2), more affectionately known as 'Nellie's'. This historic inn has five rooms with gaslighting, stone-flagged floors and often all the rooms have coal fires blazing away. Folk and traditional jazz can be heard upstairs in the function room on Monday and Wednesday evenings and there is a courtyard for summer drinking. The only cask beer is **Samuel Smith Old Brewery Bitter**. Good value home-made lunches are served except on Mondays. 'Nellie's' is now approved as a place where civil weddings can take place.

The next pub, the **Royal Standard** (3), is reached by a short walk down Hengate, alongside the impressive 14th-century

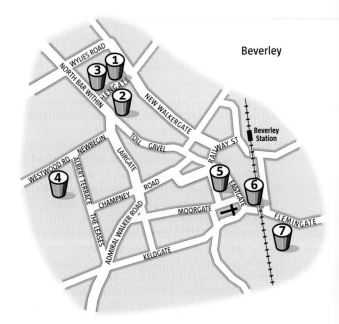

Beverley

St Mary's Church and turning right into North Bar Within.
Go towards the historic brick archway known as North Bar,
(built in 1409 at a cost of £96.0s. 11d.), and you will find the
Standard on your right next to Burgess's ice cream parlour.
It is a classic town local featuring an unspoilt front bar with
1920s bentwood seating and a match-boarded ceiling and a
comfortable lounge at the back. Beers on sale are **Tetley
Bitter** and usually **Jennings Cumberland Ale**, **Bateman XXXB**
and a guest. Food is not served but you may bring your own
sandwiches.

Retrace your steps to St Mary's Church, cross the road,
and turn right into the narrow Wood Lane which is
protected by a metal bollard. Walk up this residential street
and note the former Blue Bell Inn at No 25, a one-time beer
house that closed in the 1940s. At the junction with St Mary's
Terrace turn left, and then right into Westwood Road. The
Woolpack (4) is up on the left. It is a short walk from here to
the Westwood. The pub has recently undergone a sensitive

renovation. It was originally two cottages built around 1825 and was first licensed as a Hull Brewery house. The pub was sensitively restored in 2001 by the **Burtonwood Brewery** that now owns it. On sale are the company's **Bitter** and **Top Hat** and a monthly guest beer. The cosy snug has been retained, and tasty home-made meals are served at lunchtimes and weekday evenings.

The walk to the next pub is the longest on the crawl but takes you through the historic town centre. So, head back to St Mary's Terrace, into Newbegin with its substantial Georgian houses; cross Lairgate into a narrow passageway turning right through Saturday Market which, as the name implies, holds a popular market every Saturday. Continue through the market to the Hawkshead and Burton's building and along Toll Gavel to Skelton's bakery into Butcher Row towards Wednesday Market. From here cross into Highgate, passing Larard's estate agency.

Follow this cobbled street to the **Monk's Walk** (5), previously known by the less gimmicky name of George and Dragon. The 18th-century frontage hides two timber-framed buildings that are separated by a former medieval street leading to the nearby Friary. The bar area was refurbished in 2001 following fire damage in a pseudo-medieval theme. A brick archway at the end of the bar leads to an impressive dining room with medieval roof timbers and a log fire. Beers on draught include **Castle Eden**, **Greene King Old Speckled Hen**, **Marston's Pedigree** and a guest.

On leaving the pub bear left towards the famous Minster which, if time allows, is well worth a visit. Otherwise turn left, along the side of the Minster (noticing the Friary buildings straight ahead), and walk around the corner, crossing over the road to the **Sun Inn** (6). This medieval timber-framed building is reputed to be the town's oldest pub. Its spartan interior, with flagstone floors and bare brick walls, only dates from 1994 when it became a Tap and Spile outlet. Beers include **Black Sheep Best Bitter**, **Taylor Landlord**, **York Yorkshire Terrier** and several guest ales. Good value meals are served every day up to 8 pm except on Tuesdays.

On leaving the pub turn left and cross over the railway – you are now entering Beverley's East End. Continue along Flemingate for a couple of hundred yards and on the right is **Hodgson's** (7) opposite the Museum of Army Transport and next to the leisure centre. This imposing Georgian residence was converted during the last century into a sports and social club for Hodgson's Tannery and, after years of dilapidation it was then renovated to become a pub in 1997. This is the only free house in the town selling a selection of micro-brewery beers. The front tap room has a traditional feel in contrast to the open-plan food/disco/games area to the rear although this does feature Beverley's only skittle alley. There is good value food and a carvery is available from Thursday to Sunday.

It is only a short walk back to the railway station through Chantry Lane. To reach the bus station, go back to the Sun Inn and proceed along Eastgate, Butcher Row and Walkergate.

White Horse Inn (Nellie's), Beverley

ASK WHERE THE
White Horse is
and a few folk in
Beverley can tell you.
Ask where Nellie's is
and almost
everybody
will know.
It is the
same pub
and was run by

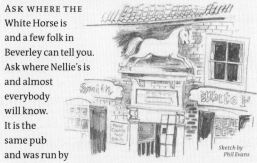

Sketch by
Phil Evans

the Collinson family from 1888 until the death of Miss Nellie
in 1976, when it was bought by the Samuel Smith Brewery
of Tadcaster. Thankfully the new owners made only
minimal changes. It remains gaslit although when Smith's
acquired it, repairs to gas pipes in the cellar made with
chewing gum were found and candles lay alongside. Drinks
were originally served from a plain marble-topped table
and the present bar is just one of the few improvements by
Smith's. In the old days when the bar became too crowded
the overflow went into the kitchen.

Nellie was a real character. She had a live-in lover known
affectionately as 'Suitcase Johnny' from the number of times
she kicked him out of the place. It was essentially a man's
pub and when the law changed to outlaw sex discrimination
a brave young woman reportedly went in and ordered a
half of bitter. Miss Collinson told her that she knew all
about the law but as long as she was in charge she wasn't
serving women. 'Get out!' she declared. Later she relented
but women were confined to one of the snugs and were not
permitted to buy drinks.

The building dates from the 15th century and although
it has not been a pub all the time since then, it was one of
Beverley's principal coaching inns. The nearby St Mary's
Church owned it until it was sold to Francis Collinson in
1928. Nellie was his daughter.

Calder and Hebble bus trail

HERE'S A BUS ROUTE on which there are lots of great pubs and which is relatively inexpensive to use – the 278 and 279 from Wakefield to Halifax *Arriva* service. There are some other services which cover parts of the route. You can buy an *Arriva* Day Ticket for £3.20 which gives unlimited travel on *Arriva* buses in West Yorkshire (they are even cheaper at weekends). Metro Day Rover Tickets can be bought in advance from bus stations and post offices and allow you to use trains and other bus operators. Buses are half-hourly up to 3.40 pm and hourly after that. Obtain a timetable by phoning Metro on 0113 245 7676 or visiting the website www.wymetro.com.

Opening times are not given as these are liable to change, so your best bet is to check by phoning the pub. The crawl could start at Wakefield bus station in Providence Street. However, you may want to sample the delights of the city centre and a short crawl of *Good Beer Guide* entries follows. Start at the **Fernandes Brewery Tap** (01924 369547) in Avisons Yard just off Kirkgate where a tourist guide-post points to the brewery. This usually has two or three of its

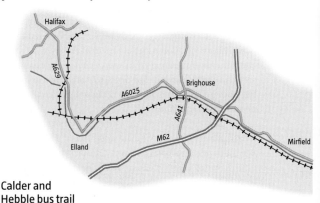

Calder and
Hebble bus trail

own beers together with guest ales and a good selection of Belgian beers and gins.

In nearby Vicarage Street, a back street off to your right just above Woolworth's, you will find **Wakefield Labour Club** (01924 215626), known as the Red Shed because that is precisely what it is. It specialises in beers from small independent brewers and bottled Belgian beers. This is a members' club but you can be signed-in as a visitor if you show a CAMRA membership card or a copy of this guide or the *Good Beer Guide*.

Head west along George Street (look out for Sainsbury's or the Royal Mail sorting office) to **O'Donoghues** (01924 291326). This is not a fake Irish pub and you can expect to find live musicians in it. There are five hand pumps and usually two of them dispense **Ossett** beers. It only opens from 5 pm except on Sundays which has all-day opening.

Quite nearby, with the address of 107B Westgate, but actually tucked away in a yard behind Bretton Hall College's Powerhouse Theatre, is a tiny gem, **Harry's Bar** (01924 373773). This friendly one-roomed pub has lots of rugby league memorabilia and offers at least four cask beers including **Clark's** beers and **Taylor Best Bitter**. There is no juke box or one-armed bandit but occasional live music.

After Harry's you will have no trouble making your way on to Westgate, where you can choose whether to try the better pubs on the famous Westgate Run such as **Henry Boon's**, the brewery tap for **Clark's Brewery**, the **Swan With Two Necks**, the **Wagon**, the **White Hart** or finally the cosy four-roomed **Redoubt**, or you can hop on to your 278/9.

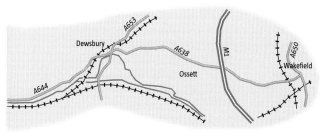

Your first stop could be just up the hill from the Morrison's superstore. Go right at the traffic lights for the **Flanshaw Hotel** (01924 290830). At first sight it is just an estate pub, but it is a good one, open all day, and with lots of community activities. Four cask ales including two regularly-changing guest beers are served in over-sized lined glasses ensuring you get a full pint.

Another choice is to get out of town and take a 15-minute ride to Flushdyke on the outskirts of Ossett for the **Red Lion** on Dewsbury Road (01924 273487). This 18th-century inn usually has four guest beers alongside **John Smith's Bitter**. It is now also home to the area's newest micro, the **Red Lion Brewery**. Good food is available but on Sundays it does tend to take over the pub.

In another ten minutes you will find yourself in Dewsbury bus station which has clean toilets, a bookstall, food and a travel centre. From here you follow signs leading uphill to the railway station, a Grade II listed Building (1848) with a waiting room that is now the **West Riding Licensed Refreshment Rooms** (01924 459193). It's a brilliant concept and a popular stop-over with rail travellers. There is innovative lunchtime food as well as curry and pie nights during the week and all-day breakfasts on Sundays, music events in the summer, jazz sessions and at least six interesting cask ales including one from the **Anglo Dutch Brewery**.

Continue to the right along this stretch of the ring road to its junction with Webster Hill A644, into the **John F Kennedy** (01924 455828), a surprising gem of a pub serving **Taylor Landlord** and a guest ale usually from the **Glentworth Brewery**. It is best to check in advance the pub's opening hours which are rather limited.

Take the bus a couple of stops out of Dewsbury along the Huddersfield Road to West Town then head left down Fall Lane and go under the railway bridge. You will find the **Gate Inn** on Thornhill Road (01924 461897). It is an unspoilt traditional three-roomed pub serving **Tetley Bitter** and a guest ale. This pub opens from 4 pm Mondays to Thursdays and from 12 noon from Fridays to Sundays.

Back on the Huddersfield Road and it is about a ten-minute journey to Mirfield. Turn left past the Lidl superstore on Station Road to find the **Navigation Inn** (01924 492476). You will see it across the canal before you reach it along a lane just before the station. It has **Theakston Best Bitter**, **Greene King Old Speckled Hen** and a house beer called **Caspers**. You could also try the **Railway** on the main Huddersfield Road (01924 480868) which has a rotating guest beer.

A few minutes' ride from Mirfield brings you to Battye Ford and the **Wilsons Arms** (01924 492217) which sells the refreshing malty **Burtonwood Bitter** and occasional guest ales. The alternative 250 or 258 routes bring you close to another pub worth visiting; the **Wasp's Nest** (01924 492352) on Nab Lane which is also reachable from the Huddersfield Road by a cobbled woody lane called Francis Street at the foot of Stocks Bank Road. It has up to seven hand pumps. Opening times vary so check.

Fifteen minutes further on through a changing, more majestically Pennine landscape brings you to Brighouse. Alight at the bus station and double back behind it along Bethel Street where you will find the **Richard Oastler**, (01484 401756) an imposing and intriguing Wetherspoon house, formerly a cathedral-scale non-conformist chapel. The beers are reasonably priced. The river bridge is a handsome piece of ironwork looking down into what is almost a gorge.

(Between Brighouse and Elland the 278 bus takes a different route along the south side of the valley, climbing through Rastrick and Lower Edge before taking a breathtaking descent into Elland. This is one of the most spectacular valley views in West Yorkshire. An alternative is to walk along the canal towpath.)

A few minutes' ride on a 279 bus takes you to the edge of Brighouse to Brookfoot where the 279 bus stops right outside the legendary **Red Rooster** (01484 713737). This popular pub stocks **Black Sheep Best Bitter**, **Rooster's Yankee** and up to five guest beers. As a novelty two-pint glasses are available.

The journey towards Elland takes you to the **Colliers Arms** (01422 372007) next to a lock on the Calder and Hebble Navigation. The collier in question is a coal barge, although the coal industry has long since disappeared from this part of the county. It sells **Samuel Smith Old Brewery Bitter** at an old-fashioned price.

A few minutes further up the road is the imposing **Barge and Barrel** (01422 373623), a substantial, unspoilt Victorian building originally built for the now departed railway, with several rooms wrapped around a horseshoe-shaped bar. There are usually beers from the local brewer **Eastwood & Sanders** alongside guest beers as well as real cider and perry. Food is served from Tuesdays to Saturdays. You can relax here with a daily newspaper.

From Elland it is about a 15-minute run into Halifax, but there are a couple of pubs on the way that are worth visiting. They are the **Falcon Inn** (01422 365077) in Salterhebble with two cask ales, and the **Stafford Arms** in Huddersfield Road, which sells **Taylor Landlord**.

On arriving in Halifax it is advisable not to go all the way to the bus station but better to get off on Skircoat Road close to the Shay Football Ground. Then cross the road, go down Hunger Hill then left on to the wider South Parade. Turn left and a few dozen yards up the hill is the **Three Pigeons** (01422 347001). It is an unspoilt 1930s Art Deco, multi-roomed but cosy boozer with around seven cask ales available with many from Yorkshire micros and a choice of 30 different rums. It is a popular finishing point and if you don't know anyone when you go into the pub then that's unlikely to be the case for long!

Do you really want another pub? Well, just across the road on the left is the **Pump Room** (01422 381465), which offers up to ten cask ales and is a regular outlet for the **Ossett Brewery**.

Masham

Not so much a pub crawl, more a lesson in brewing

MASHAM ranks as joint number two in Yorkshire's brewing towns with two medium-sized breweries and both of them have visitor centres which makes a pub crawl of the town something different – four excellent pubs with a total choice of around a dozen beers – and two breweries. It is an attractive town with the largest market square in the county and the splendid 11th-century church of St Mary has a wonderful 20th-century Madonna and Child painting on display. And the nooks and crannies of Masham are well worth exploring too. There is a down turn and that is the lack of public transport with only a few buses each day linking the town with Ripon to the south and Bedale, Leyburn and Richmond northwards. However there is plenty of accommodation so that a car journey before the pub crawl and a good night's sleep after it seems a good idea.

Start in the square with a pint or two in the **King's Head** (1) a residential hotel (01765 689295) owned by Theakston's that stands out in a collection of handsome buildings in the market square. This fine Georgian building has in its time also been a posting house and for a while the excise office. It is splendidly old-fashioned, decked out in wood, with an entrance hall that leads to the two main rooms. On the right is a fine dining hall with some large family tables and the main bar that is to the left has an open area and several alcoves. In fine weather you can drink in the coach yard with fairy lights in the evenings. The hotel opens all day and on the bar are **Theakston** beers, usually **Old Peculier**, **Black Bull Bitter**, **Best Bitter** and **XB** with a guest ale. The food is first class and reasonably priced and served all day.

Turn left on leaving and from the west side of the square follow the signs for the **Theakston Brewery Visitor Centre** (2). It is only a few minutes' walk passing some of the delightful old houses that grace this pleasant town. It carries an imposing sign of the Black Bull in Paradise as the brewery

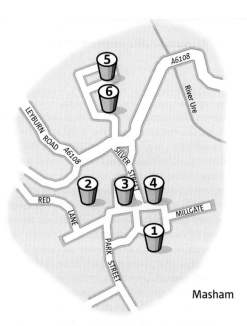

Masham

was once in the yard of the Black Bull Inn in Paradise Fields.
The centre includes an excellent exhibition of brewing tools
and materials and a room devoted to traditional pub games.
There are audio-visual presentations of brewing and of the
cooperage – one of very few still operating in British
breweries. Occasionally visitors are asked to try their hand
at making a wooden barrel. There is also a gift shop. There
are also brewery tours after which visitors receive samples
of the company's brews. It opens daily from 10.30 am to
4.30 pm with tours on the hour from 11 am. The cost is
£4.50 with concessions. Full details can be obtained from
01765 680000 or on the website at **www.theakstons.co.uk**.
And the good news is that just before the publication of
this guide the brewery is once more in the ownership of the
Theakston family.

When you leave the centre turn left and follow signs for
the Market Place. This route takes you through an area of
old cottages and workshops and brings you into Silver Street.

Turn right and go past two traditional shops that are worth looking at – a grocery and a butcher – to the **Bay Horse** (3). Two wooden-floored rooms open out from a central corridor with the one on the left dedicated to games and decorated with a sporting theme. The main bar has comfortable settles and lots of local interest. There is also a small pool room and tables on the forecourt. On the hand pulls are **Theakston Best Bitter**, **Black Sheep Best Bitter** and **Special** and **John Smith's Bitter**. The pub opens all day and food is served from 11 am to 2 pm and from 4 pm to 8 pm except on Fridays when there is no break in service.

Cross the road into Little Market Square and on the left is the **Bruce Arms** (4). Here's a warning before you enter: turn off any mobile phones for there is a fine of one pound for any that ring in the pub. It all goes to local charities and in 2002 raised £600. The pub divides easily into three areas: on the right is mainly for dining, the bar and entrance is in the centre and there is a larger room to the left with a wood-burning fire dedicated to games – with its own darts alley. There is loads of interest with framed cigarette cards, old advertisements and local pictures. It sells **John Smith's Bitter**, **Tetley Bitter**, **Black Sheep Best Bitter** and a guest ale in summer. Meals are served at lunchtimes and in the evenings on Wednesdays, Thursdays, Saturdays and Sundays. Bed and breakfast is available (01765 689372).

Turn right out of the pub and then right into Silver Street and turn your mobile phone on – if you must! At the fork go left and cross the main road and keep left following the signs for the **Black Sheep Brewery Visitor Centre** (5). It opens daily from 10 am to 5 pm with tours around the brewery at 11.30 am, 12.30 pm, 2 pm and 3 pm and at 4 pm if there is a demand. It costs £4.50 with concessions including a family ticket at £9.95 for two adults and up to four children. Admission to the bistro, which opens until 11 pm from Wednesdays to Sundays, and the shop and bar area is free. **Black Sheep Best Bitter**, **Special**, **Riggwelter** and seasonal specials are on sale. You can obtain full details on 01765 689227 or the website at www.blacksheepbrewery.com.

Retrace your steps and turn left into Crosshills for the **White Bear** (6) a free house that backs on to one brewery and is next door to the offices of another. Despite its obvious age it only dates as a pub from 1941 when its predecessor was destroyed by a stray German bomb. Beautifully florally decked out in summer this pub is one to sit outside if the weather allows. Inside it maintains a separate public bar in which the eponymous animal smiles down on the customers from the comfort of its glass case; the bear was shot in Alaska in 1901 by Mr J C Lister – whoever he may have been. The lounge is a good place to eat and the food, available lunchtimes and evenings except on Sundays when lunches only are served, is excellent value. The pub opens all day. On the bars are beers from **Theakston**: **Best Bitter**, **Black Bull Bitter** and **Old Peculier**, the prize-winning **Caledonian Deuchars IPA** and a guest beer. There are occasional traditional jazz nights.

A walk back to the Market Square or wherever you may be headed cannot be anything but pleasant in this most delightful of Yorkshire towns.

Theakston's Brewery, Masham

Scarborough
The Queen of the watering places

> *The evening closed in with the most glorious sunset ever*
> *witnessed. The castle on the cliff stood in proud glory,*
> *gilded by the rays of the declining sun. The distant ships*
> *glittered like burnished gold. The little boats near the*
> *beach heaved on the ebbing tide, inviting occupants.*
> *The view was grand beyond description.* ELLEN NUSSEY

SCARBOROUGH was founded more than ten centuries ago
although there is evidence of a Roman signal station there
from the 4th century. Its origins as a spa date from 1620 but
'taking of the waters' ceased in 1939. The spa complex on
the south bay remains as a venue for entertainment and
conferences. The town is Yorkshire's premier seaside resort
with a popularity that does not diminish. Its road pattern is
Victorian, its style still captures the traditional and the folk
are open, free thinking and happy to welcome visitors.
And the pubs, as in most resorts, are a mixed lot, either
with a particular customer in mind or possibly eclectic and
it is from this latter grouping that this crawl is based.

It is a linear crawl and if your journey is by rail then it is
best to start at the far end which is not more than three
quarters of a mile from the railway station, where it finishes.
Or you might care to take a taxi. Walk down Westborough
which becomes Newborough and in the precinct turn left
into St Thomas Street. Cross Castle Road into North Marine
Road and at the far end on the right, opposite the county
cricket ground is, appropriately, the **Cricketers** (1). The
views across North Bay and the castle are magnificent and
make a suitable accompaniment to the fine portfolio of
beers: **Taylor Landlord**, **Tetley Bitter**, **York Yorkshire Terrier** and
a changing variety of guest ales. The food is good too with
meals served all day, every day up to 9pm. There is a large
family room upstairs with entertainment for children
during the summer. Although it is said to be Scarborough's
best-kept secret, the pub can get busy during match days –

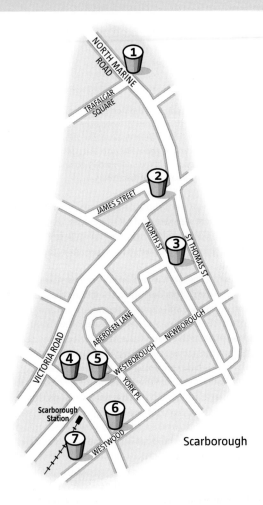

Scarborough

Yorkshire play several games here and there are other first-class matches too.

Retrace your steps, crossing the road for **Indigo Alley** (2) which is a fine example of a run down and eventually closed pub being brought back to life with a simple make-over and a name change. It is now a popular and busy local that has won several awards in its comparatively short renaissance. On the taps are six constantly-changing guest ales and a Belgian beer. Live music is performed four nights each week and there is also the occasional play. It opens at 4 pm but earlier at weekends.

Turn right into Castle Road and left into North Street and on the right near to the end is the **Angel** (3), one of the town's smallest pubs. It sells **Tetley Bitter** and **Camerons Bitter** and bar food at lunchtimes. It has a rugby league theme with pictures and memorabilia.

Go on past the post office in Aberdeen Walk and along Westborough to Alma Parade for the **Alma Inn** (4), a friendly pub with a comfortable lounge and a cosy back bar. It sells beers from the local **Malton Brewery** along with **Tetley Bitter**, **Theakston Best Bitter** and guest beers. Lunches are served.

Around the corner in Westborough is the **Lord Roseberry** (5) a Wetherspoon conversion from the fine 19th-century building that was formerly the town's Liberal club. There are two bars on the ground and upper floors which sell **Courage Directors**, **Theakston Best Bitter**, **Shepherd Neame Spitfire** and interesting guest beers. Food is served up to 8pm. There is no TV or canned music.

Cross over Westborough and go down York Place, turning right into Somerset Terrace for the **Scholars Bar** (6). It is part of the Bedford Hotel and the bar has been recently extended and now carries four hand pumps serving a constantly-changing range of beers mainly from small breweries in Yorkshire and Durham. It closes during weekday afternoons in winter but is otherwise open all day and food is served until early evenings.

Turn right into Valley Bridge Road to return to the railway station. In here in the former refreshment room is the **Head of Steam** (7), your final call. The beer range varies but there are usually beers from the **Caledonian** and **Black Sheep** breweries, one local beer and maybe another guest. It hosts regular beer festivals with regional themes such as Shropshire, Ireland, the south-west. The food is excellent here and is served into the early evening. It is part of a small group of pubs on or close to railway stations and consequently there is lots of railwayania.

Your train awaits.

IT'S PLEASANT TO the taste, strong and mellow,
he that effects it not is no boon fellow;
He that in this drink doth let his senses swim,
there's neither wind nor storm will pierce him,
It warms in winter, in summer opes the pores,
'twill make a sovereign salve 'gainst cuts and sores;
It ripens wit, excelerates the mind,
makes friends of foes, and foes of friends full kind;
It's physical for old men, warms their blood,
It's spirit makes the cowards courage good;
The tatter'd beggar, being warm'd with ale
nor rain, hail, frost, nor snow can him assail;
He's a good man with him can then compare,
it makes a'prentice great as the Lord Mayor;
The labouring man that toils all day full sore,
a pot of ale at night does him restore,
and makes him all his toils and pains forget,
and for another day-work he's then fit.
There's more in drinking ale sure than we wot,
for most ingenious artists love a pot:
Soldiers and Gownmen,
rich and poor, old and young, lame and sound men,
may such advantage reap by drinking ale,
as should I tell you think it but a tale.

From *The Praise of Yorkshire Ale,* George Meriton

Black Sheep Brewery, Masham

Scotland

IT MAY SEEM PRESUMPTUOUS for an Englishman to write about Scotland, but I can say in all honesty that every visit I have made there has been enjoyable and well worth while. It has fantastic scenery, marvellous architecture, and a cultural tradition second to none. And, of late, I have enjoyed the pubs – let's call them bars to be more accurate – particularly in the great cities.

It is far too vast a country to examine in any detail in so few words. The beauty and grandeur of the Highlands and Islands contrast with the splendour of the buildings of Aberdeen, Dundee, Edinburgh and Glasgow and between and around are so many other delights particularly on its thousands of miles of coastline. And there's golf too.

Thirty years ago the pub and beer scene was dire. In the 1974 *Good Beer Guide* there were no entries at all for Scotland. The following year, timorously, just over 50 were noted. Nowadays there are more than 300 with many more anxious to make the grade. Ten breweries have grown to 30. And what wonderful bars and beers there are as the three crawls in this section will show.

Dumfries

Then let us toast John Barleycorn,
Each man a glass in hand;
And may his great posterity
Ne'er fail in old Scotland.

ROBERT BURNS

DUMFRIES is a popular town because of its connections
with Scotland's patriot bard Robert Burns and this pub
crawl has a Burns theme. We start at the railway station
where trains from Newcastle, Carlisle, Glasgow and other
Scottish stations call. Depending on the time of your visit
you can choose to do the crawl in reverse visiting the Ship
first as it closes in the afternoons.

Walk along Newall Terrace and in the town centre
turn right into Queensberry Street and on the left is the
Tam O'Shanter (1). This is a 17th-century former coaching inn
whose name comes from one of Burns' most famous poems
Tam O'Shanter in which he glorified the inn. This is an old-
fashioned pub with a partition in the bar, three small rooms
and little altered over the years. A half-panelled corridor
runs down the left side and there is a wee no-smoking
room to the right with a curtained entrance. This was
originally the kitchen and has a splendid range fireplace.
The walls here have been painted red and on them are
some of Burns' poems. The back room is carpeted and
another small room has upholstered benches and brewery
mirrors. On sale are **Caledonian Deuchars IPA**, **Belhaven 80/-**
and two guest beers usually from Scottish micro-breweries.
It opens all day with food served from noon to 4 pm.

Turn left out of the pub and left towards the pedestrian
area and on your right at the corner of Castle Street and
Buccleuch Street is the **Robert the Bruce** (2). Wetherspoon's
converted it in part from a Methodist church. Basically
open-plan the former church part has a high ceiling and
there is also a mezzanine floor. It opens all day with food
served up to 10 pm. Beers on sale are **Caledonian Deuchars**

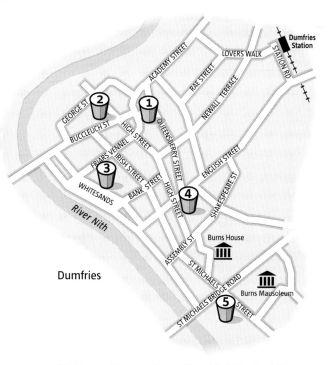

Dumfries

IPA, **Courage Directors**, **Greene King Abbot**, **Shepherd Neame Spitfire** and two guests.

Walk down Buccleuch Street and left alongside the River Nith and shortly you will find the **New Bazaar** (3) on Whitesands. This Victorian sandstone pub has a splendid old-fashioned carved gantry in the bar. Look out for the lower marble shelf and some 200 malt whiskies. Cask beers on offer are **McEwan's 80/-**, **Belhaven St Andrew's Ale**, **Sulwath Knockendoch** from nearby Castle Douglas and usually two guest ales. A doorway leads to the small and smart lounge on the right with a coal fire and there is also a meeting room at the rear. It opens all day from 11 am to 11 pm with an extension to midnight from Thursdays to Saturdays.

Continue along the riverside and turn left up Bank Street and right into High Street and on the left is the entrance to the **Globe** (4) known locally as Burns Howff.

It is internationally famous for its Robert Burns connections. On the bar are **Caledonian Deuchars IPA** and **Bards Ale** which elsewhere is known as **Belhaven 80/-**. The pub opens all day from 10 am with late opening from Thursdays to Sundays. Breakfasts and lunches are served except on Sundays.

Turn left back into High Street and if after leaving the Globe you want to find out more about Robert Burns walk into Burns Street and visit the Robert Burns House where he spent the last years of his life. It opens every day from April to September but closes Sundays and Mondays in winter. Admission is free.

Burns Street leads to St Michaels Street and across the main road is the final resting place of Burns. His mausoleum is in the churchyard of St Michael's. Opposite is a splendid traditional pub, the Grade B listed, **Ship** (5). It has two rooms where conversation and good beer predominate. There is no piped music, no machines, no pool, no darts, no food, only crisps and nuts, no keg or smooth beer, no cigarette machine and the TV in the lounge is only occasionally used for major football matches. There are also original pub hours with afternoon closing. On the front are two good stained and leaded windows featuring a ship in the centre and the inner door has a 'Ship Inn' etched and frosted window. The main bar is a long and narrow room with good half panelling running from side to side rather than the usual up and down style. The gantry has a mirrored back with a number of shelves but the highlight is the excellent ceiling plasterwork with deep cut cornices and two amazing decorative ceiling roses. There is a lounge at the rear with another excellent ceiling rose and superb cornice work.

The pub has a wide range of beers with **McEwan's 80/-** and the rare **Belhaven 60/-** (also known as 'light') served in the traditional Scottish way by air compressor fonts. There are four in all and unusually they are situated below the level of the bar. Up to six real ales are served on hand pump including **Greene King Abbot**, **Marston's Pedigree** and **Taylor Landlord**.

To return to the station go back to the main road and turn right into Brooms Road opposite the fire station and then left into Leafield Road. Go across Annan Road, turn right and Station Road is a short way along on the left.

The Globe Inn, Burns Howff

THE GLOBE has been owned by the McKerrow family since 1937. Enter it down the narrow wynd (alley) and into a short passage. On the busy days of summer there are tours at 10.30 am, 3 pm and 7 pm but they try to accommodate anyone who is interested. You can ring the pub in advance on 01387 252335. The manager, Jane Brown, is a Burns' enthusiast and she provides an excellent guided tour.

The lounge bar has been extended into former stabling. The long, narrow room has a lot of pew-style benches and upholstered chairs. The wood-panelled, tiny snug bar has a sliding door, wood panelling all around and bare wooden benches attached. There is a good bar front with a water tap on the bar and a number of framed prints on the walls.

The splendid Burns room at the front end of the pub still has the bard's favourite carved chair by the stone fireplace with its bucket-style log fire. If you sit in the chair you must recite a line of Burns or your penalty is to buy all the customers in the bar a drink. The wood-panelled walls date from 1780 and there are two display cases and framed items of Burns memorabilia. Above the fireplace is a mural of Burns and his plough. There is a curved cupboard near the door that can seat 16 at a push and can be booked for a special evening complete with a Piper playing a lament.

The tour continues up the tartan carpeted staircase and a large old-fashioned key opens the Burns bedroom with its lovely cast fireplace and a four-poster bed. The two statues on the mantelshelf are of Jean Armour Burns and Robert Burns. Two of the window panes have etched verses made with a diamond which have been authenticated as the poet's writings. The Howff Club Room at the rear was discovered in 1937. It is wood panelled and the venue for monthly meetings of the Burns Howff Club. There is a virtual tour on the website: www.globeinndumfries.co.uk.

Dundee

Beautiful railway bridge of the Silvery Tay,
Alas, I am very sorry to say,
That ninety lives have been taken away,
On the last Sabbath day of 1879,
Which will be remembered for a very long time.

WILLIAM McGONAGALL

THE BEST WAY TO SCOTLAND's fourth largest city is by railway from Edinburgh or further south. The route takes you across two of the most famous railway bridges in the whole of Britain – the impressive Forth Rail Bridge and the McGonagall lauded Tay Bridge. Dundee is an important industrial centre and port and an outlet for the North Sea oilfield. Its printing and publishing businesses are well known for their production of children's comics.

From the railway station it is a one mile walk to start the crawl by turning left and following the main road to the traffic lights. Turn left into Nethergate and keep walking up past the university in Perth Road to the **Speedwell** (1) on the right. Or, if you go by bus, take the walkway over the main road towards the city centre, turn right, then first left and walk up Whitehall Street. Travel Dundee buses 9, 9X and 11 or Strathtay buses 73 and 75 will take you to Sinderins Junction where the Perth Road meets Hawkhill Walk. Go down Perth Road and you will soon find the Speedwell on the left.

This is a splendid unaltered Edwardian gem built in 1903 for James Speed a local wine and spirit merchant that left the property to a trust. It is known as Mennies after the family that ran it for nearly 50 years from the 1920s. It has an L-shaped bar split into two by a low screen and two other separate sitting rooms on the left, one of which is no-smoking. This Grade B listed building has a splendid original gantry with many bays. There is a crafted mahogany bar, etched windows in the doors, dado panelling and ornamental ceiling, frieze and cornices. A visit to the gents

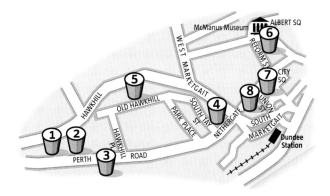

is a must to view the original Shanks fitments, crazed white tiled walls and mosaic floors. The Speedwell Tavern is one of four pubs in Dundee on CAMRA's National Inventory of Pub Interiors of Outstanding Historic Interest. It opens from 11 am to midnight except on Sundays when the hours are 12.30 pm to midnight. The beer range varies but there are always three or four cask ales which change regularly, and 160 malt whiskies including a Macallan 30 year old at £10 a nip. The only food is toasted sandwiches.

Further down Perth Road going back towards the city centre on the same side is the *Taybridge Bar* (2). This splendid unspoilt three-roomed pub with its impressive mirrored Victorian bar back, tiny snug and Art Deco lounge is also on CAMRA's National Inventory but sadly does not sell cask ales.

Cross the road to **Drouthy Neebors** (3). The name is taken from Robert Burns' famous poem *Tam O' Shanter,* written as a glorification of the inn, where drouthy (thirsty) neighbours enjoy good fellowship and foaming pints (reaming swats) of ale. On the walls are quotes from the bard's works. Formerly a motor showroom, it is on several levels and a spiral staircase leads down to the basement bar which occasionally hosts live bands. It opens all day, every day with food from noon until 8 pm. Two real ales are on the hand pulls including one from the **Inveralmond Brewery** in Perth.

Go downhill and the road becomes Nethergate and on your left is the **Phoenix** (4). The splendid gantry with deep etched mirrors and a lovely frieze on the top was salvaged from a demolished Victorian pub in Cardiff. Other features include a carved bar front, polished stone bar top, two cast iron columns holding up the splendid restored ceiling with its decorative cornice of rose symbols. At the rear is an old Guinness Time illuminated clock hanging from the ceiling. The walls are decorated with an assortment of items including old enamel signs. The single room has a quarry-tiled floor and there are a number of short partitions with stained-glass panels which help to create separate areas. The double entrance doors have stained and leaded panels and there is an attractive phoenix above them. The bar opens all day until midnight with food up to 7 pm. It sells **Orkney Dark Island**, **Taylor Landlord**, **Houston Peter's Well** and **Caledonian Deuchars IPA**.

Walk a few yards back up Nethergate turning into South Tay Street. At the end turn left and a short way up Old Hawkhill, **Mickey Coyle's** (5) is on the right. It was once called 'MC' and was in the Guinness Book of Records as the pub with the shortest name. There is one L-shaped lounge bar with a small area at a lower level. There is occasional folk music. It opens all day but only from 7 pm on Sundays.

Caledonian Deuchars IPA and **80/-** are on the hand pumps and food is available at lunchtimes and early evenings on weekdays.

Head towards the city centre and cross the dual carriageway of Marketgait, then walk along South Ward Road, Meadowside and into Albert Square. Here you will find Dundee's McManus Art Gallery and Museum. This is worth a visit if only to see the facsimile pub which features the bar from the Old Toll Lochee and hand pumps from John O'Groats, two Dundee pubs that have been demolished. Admission is free.

Across the road in Reform Street is the **Counting House** (6), a listed building that was formerly the Royal Bank of Scotland and a typical Wetherspoon conversion. Some good cornice work remains and the pub is essentially one big bar with raised carpeted areas to the left and right. It opens all day and sells food most of the time along with up to six beers including one or two **Caledonian** beers, **Courage Directors** and guests. There is a no-smoking area.

Continue along Reform Street to City Square, turn right and opposite the parish church of St Mary, on your left is Union Street. The building on the corner is the **Trades House** (7), a stunning conversion of a Bank of Scotland branch with oak panelling, marble columns, a set of handsome stained-glass windows showing various trades, engraved mirrors and leather wall seats. You enter to a wonderful mosaic floor with a shield and two dragons. There are even three snugs created by new partitions. There is music on Friday and Saturday nights but it is quiet at other times. It opens from 11 am to midnight and usually has one cask ale on sale.

Opposite is the **Bank Bar** (8), a former small TSB branch and initially a Hogshead pub. There is a splendid bar front with ecclesiastical arch patterning and the little snug has an antique settle and some partitioned seating areas. It sells **Caledonian Deuchars IPA**, **Marston's Pedigree**, **Boddingtons Bitter** and an **Inveralmond** beer. Live music nights are Thursdays and Fridays. The bar opens all day to midnight with food up to 8 pm.

A short walk down Union Street and across a walkway brings you back to the railway station.

Edinburgh

Through the Old Town

> *Edina! Scotia's darling seat,*
> *All hail thy palaces and tow'rs,*
> *Where once beneath a Monarch's feet*
> *Sat Legislation's sov'reign pow'rs.*   ROBERT BURNS

AMONGST ALL the many other things Edinburgh is renowned for throughout the world, it is also a world class drinking city with a wide variety of pubs reflecting its status as the British Empire's second city of brewing. It is also one of the last bastions of tall founts which dispense beer by the traditional Scottish air pressure method. Air dispense relies on the Venturi effect. If you are a mechanical engineer you will know what that means. If not, ask the licensee. You will notice that founts stand proud of the bar. This was for the simple reason that the customer could see his beer being poured into his glass, ensuring that no slops found their way into it courtesy of an unscrupulous landlord. This crawl celebrates tall founts and the fantastic amount of original Scottish brewery mirrors that still exist despite the fact that most of the breweries were reduced to rubble many years ago. Connoisseurs of single malt whisky will not be disappointed either as many of the pubs on the crawl have an extensive range of malts.

Our crawl is through Edinburgh's Old Town and starts at Haymarket railway station which is well served by buses and trains – it is the first stop on the line north from Waverley. Head east along West Maitland Street towards Princes Street and the third street on the left is Coates Crescent. Follow it to its apex and turn left on to Walker Street and immediately right on to William Street where **Bert's Bar** (1) is 20 yards along on the left-hand side. This was originally intended to be part of a Scotland wide chain of ale houses but is one of only two left. The hand pumps dispense **Caledonian Deuchars IPA** and **80/-**, **Tetley Burton Ale** and up to five guest beers. Whilst these come from all over Britain, the emphasis is on Scottish beers, with those from

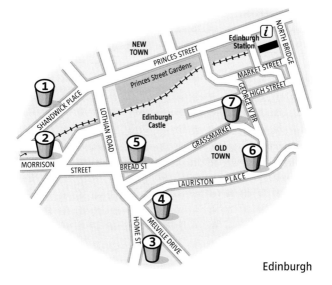

Edinburgh

the **Arran Brewery** being regularly featured. As befits a Scottish ale house there are some excellent original Scottish brewery mirrors including an absolute classic from former Edinburgh brewers Lorimer & Clark in the front room. It is open all day but closes on Sundays.

Start back towards Haymarket but at the first set of traffic lights do a U-turn on to Torphichen Street, turning immediately right on to Torphichen Place and follow it for 50 yards to the traffic lights. At the lights turn left into Morrison Street and **Thomson's Bar** (2) is 100 yards up the hill on the left-hand side. It is dedicated to the forgotten Glasgow (yes, Glasgow) architect Alexander 'Greek' Thomson. A quick glance at your surroundings will confirm where Thomson got his inspiration. The walls feature a veritable history lesson of long-closed Scottish breweries. Eight traditional Scottish tall founts dispense **Caledonian Deuchars IPA** and **80/-**, **Taylor Landlord** and up to five guest beers often including some from the **Arran**, **Atlas** and **Pictish** breweries. The pub opens all day and lunches are served Mondays to Fridays but it closes on Sundays.

175

From Thomson's turn left and follow Morrison Street until its junction with Lothian Road. Turn right and follow this road for 200 yards to Tollcross. Bear right up Leven Street past the King's Theatre to **Bennett's Bar** (3). First established in 1839, this is, architecturally, one of the top pubs in the city. Whilst a bank of tall founts adorn the bar, sadly they are no longer usable but hand pumps dispense **Caledonian Deuchars IPA** and **McEwan's 80/-**. Hot lunches are served. It opens all day but closes on Sunday lunchtimes. Drink in the atmosphere and surroundings – they don't make them like this any more.

Return to Tollcross and turn right into Brougham Street. **Cloisters Bar** (4) is about 100 yards along on the left-hand side of the street. Its name is derived from the fact that it used to be the parsonage for the adjoining All Saints Episcopal Church and it was converted into an ale house in 1995. There is another excellent collection of rare brewery mirrors and the outstanding gantry, housing upwards of 50 malts, was made from wood from a redundant church. The four regular beers are **Caledonian Deuchars IPA** and **80/-**, **Taylor Landlord** and **Greene King IPA** and five guest beers – often from **Atlas** and **Harviestoun** – and a large selection of malt whiskies are also available. It opens all day, every day and good value lunches are served. The regular beers used to be dispensed by tall fount but, sadly, this practice ceased in the summer of 2002 as they were worn out and beyond repair.

Bennett's Bar, 8 Leven Street, Edinburgh

The reason for the precise address is because there is also a Bennet's Bar in Edinburgh, both excellent in their own right and not too far from one another. But this one is on the pub crawl. And even before you enter the pub, the superb Jeffrey's Brewery etched door panels will give you an idea of what to expect inside. Four whisky barrels adorn the magnificent gantry, which houses over 100 malts, and there is a little snug bar in the corner that now serves as the telephone kiosk. There are some superb brewery mirrors with carved wood surrounds and inset tiled murals of Scottish heroes. Whilst the Bernard's mirror at the opposite end of the bar is the most spectacular, the two Taylor McLeod mirrors are the most appropriate as that brewery, which closed in the early part of the 20th century, stood on the site of what is now the nearby King's Theatre. The ceiling is elaborately moulded and the whole atmosphere is one of style, character and indulgence. It is a stunning bar.

And for the record Bennet's Bar is at 1 Maxwell Street in Morningside and is in the *Good Beer Guide*.

Return to Tollcross once more and head down Lothian Road back to the junction with Morrison Street. Turn right into Bread Street and about 200 yards along on the left-hand side is the **Blue Blazer** (5) another shrine to tall founts. At night, the bar and gantry are festooned with floating candles and the lights are turned down low, lending the bar an atmospheric touch. Since August 2003 the pub has been an official part of the annual Edinburgh Festival Fringe. There are three regular beers, with **Caledonian Deuchars IPA** and **Greene King Old Speckled Hen** being dispensed through the tall founts and **McEwan's 80/-** by hand pump, and five guests, mainly, but not exclusively, from Scottish micros.

When you leave the Blazer turn right and head down to the Grassmarket. Do not bother troubling the tills of any pubs in this area but, instead, carry on through it and turn right up Candlemaker Row passing Greyfriars Bobby's statue and into Forrest Road. Fifty yards along on the right-hand side you will find the legendary **Sandy Bell's** (6). If you like folk music this is the pub for you. At least two musicians play every night and weekend afternoons. Others turn up to play along or just sit and listen. There is no snobbery. If you bring your fiddle, chances are the regulars will happily let you play along. Four beers are on offer, **Caledonian Deuchars IPA**, **Courage Directors**, **McEwan's 80/-** and a guest ale.

Head back to Greyfriars Bobby's statue, this time keeping it on your left and head along George IV Bridge. Immediately after the Central Library turn left down Victoria Street and halfway down, on the left-hand side is the **Bow Bar** (7). This is the original ale house that spawned hundreds of second-rate imitators like Hogsheads. It is a one-roomed basic bar with a fine collection of mirrors, advertising signs and loads of atmosphere made all the better by no piped music. Tall founts dispense **Caledonian Deuchars IPA** and **80/-**, **Belhaven 80/-**, **Taylor Landlord** and four interesting guest beers. More than 150 single malt whiskies are available – ask the staff to see the list. Food is plain – mainly rolls and pies. It opens all day, every day.

Head back up Victoria Street and turn left on to George IV Bridge again. The next road junction is the Royal Mile, the heart of the World Heritage site that is Edinburgh's Old Town.

Scottish shilling terminology

THE TRADITIONAL method of categorising Scottish beers, at least from 1880 when beer duty replaced sugar and malt tax, was by way of the shilling terminology. Under this system, beers were categorised by price per barrel in order of ascending strength. Most breweries produced beers ranging from very weak Table and Harvest Beers of 28/- and 36/-, Light and Mild Beers of 42/- and 48/-, Pale Ales of 54/- and 60/-, Export and Imperial ales of 70/- and 80/-, right up to Strong Ales of Twelve and Fifteen Guineas, on top of which a range of stouts and porters would be brewed.

The ales at the strongest end of the range were very potent, and were usually sold in bottle form in 'nips' of one third of an imperial pint. 'Nips' were known as Wee Heavy beers, a term peculiar to Scotland, as indeed was the whole shilling terminology itself.

It must be stressed that the shilling system was only an invoice price, the real price being determined by taking into account both beer duty and discounts offered by the brewers, which in some cases could be substantial, amounting to as much as 50 per cent of the cost of a barrel. Hence the invoice price was only an indication of the type of beer, the real price being determined by the size and amount of the discount and duties.

To further complicate matters, this terminology was applied not only to barrels of 36 gallons, but also to hogsheads of 54 gallons and sometimes to larger containers also. Thus what in a barrel was 60/- Ale, became in a hogshead 90/- Ale, although this was exactly the same beer.

From *Beer – a Proud Tradition*
(Scottish Drink Book), Charles McMaster

Wales

MOUNTAINS AND THE SEA, male-voice choirs, eisteddfod, coal and rugby – they are all as essentially Welsh as the nation's own language. The cities of the south were the crucial links with the coal and steel industries and the resorts of the coasts were the lungs for the workers in these heavy industries. Yet four-fifths of the Princedom remains agricultural land topped by the steadfast and stately mountains.

The decline of industry has to some extent been replaced with an upsurge in the financial services market, the development of light industries and particularly in tourism where European money and foreign investment has brought in better communications and travel opportunities.

Wales has had a sad history in the pub business with Sunday closing and a strong tee-total tradition linked with its non-conformist culture. However, things have changed considerably and greater accessibility to responsible drinking and improvements in the pub estate has been mirrored by a stream of new small breweries that now tops 30.

There are three crawls for Wales, all in holiday areas, with one in the south and two on the north coast including one that uses public transport throughout.

Bay of Colwyn

THIS STRETCH of the North Wales coastline links holiday resorts that were born in the early Victorian era with the coming of the railway. The crawl follows the main coast road and promenade from Rhos-on-Sea through Colwyn Bay to Old Colwyn. It also keeps close to a bus route – the Arriva No 12 – which runs three to four times an hour during the day and half-hourly in the evening between Llandudno and Rhyl. The Holyhead to London railway line parallels the main road as does National Cycle Route 5 which is also a pedestrian way. Colwyn Bay railway station is roughly in the middle of the crawl.

The crawl starts on the promenade at Rhos-on-Sea at the **Rhos Fynach** (1) an attractive free house which was built on the site of an old monastery and is reputedly the oldest building in the area. It serves mainly **Banks's** beers including guest beers from their list and is open all permitted hours.

Go eastwards along the promenade and take in the view over the small harbour until you reach the **Cayley Arms** (2) on the right. Pop in if you fancy a pint of **Draught Bass** as this will be your only chance on this crawl. At the side of the Cayley Arms walk a short distance up Rhos Road then turn

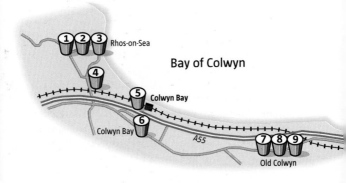

left into Everard Road to the **Boat House Club** (3) which opens all day and serves excellent **Mansfield Dark Mild** and **Cask Ale**.

Return to the promenade and continue east for about three quarters of a mile enjoying the magnificent coastal scenery and, hopefully, the delightfully bracing air until you reach the **Toad Hall** (4). This is a Wolverhampton & Dudley tied house serving a range of **Banks's**, **Mansfield** and **Marston's** beers. There are impressive views over the bay from the promenade level patio and the upstairs bar and there is a cosy restaurant at the rear. It opens at 12 noon and is closed in the afternoons.

Continue along the promenade and turn right up Marine Road under the railway and A55 then left along Princes Drive until you reach the **Picture House** (5). This is a typical Wetherspoon's pub with no fruit machines or juke boxes and a no-smoking area. The drink selection will depend on the day but will include three basic beers and four changing guests. Food is available all day.

Across the road and opposite the railway station forecourt is the **Wings Club** (6) that serves excellent and reasonably-priced **Lees GB Mild** and **Bitter**. The entrance is the door next to the Tourist Information Centre, up a flight of stairs then along a corridor. It is a social club where visitors are welcome – particularly CAMRA members, as the club is very proud that it was CAMRA Club of the Year in 2000. There is snooker, pool, darts and live entertainment. The club closes in the afternoons.

The next call is in Old Colwyn, about two and a half miles eastward. Two routes are available – either go by bus or walk or cycle along the promenade. By bus turn right out of the Wings Club then right again into Station Road. At the top of Station Road catch any eastbound bus from outside the Central (a Bass pub that no longer sells real ale) going to Old Colwyn and ask to be put off at the Plough.

If walking (about 30 to 40 minutes) you will experience more of the wonderful coastal scenery. Return to the promenade and go east, that is turn right, and continue to its end. Turn right, under the railway, then right again and up Beach Road. Follow this, with the picturesque stream running alongside, until you reach the main road.

Opposite, and a little to the right, is the **Plough** (7). This is an Inn Partnership pub selling **Boddingtons Bitter** and **Greenalls Bitter** and usually two guest ales. Food is available every lunchtime. It is the watering-hole of the local male voice choir. The pub closes in the afternoons.

Turn right and 100 yards along Abergele Road you will find the **Sun** (8) another Wolverhampton & Dudley tied house that serves a range of **Banks's**, **Mansfield** and **Marston's** beers and, often, an independent guest ale. It opens lunchtimes and evenings.

Next door you will find the famed **Red Lion** (9) which only opens in the evenings during the week but all day at weekends. There is an interesting range of beers including **Boddingtons Bitter**, **Flowers Original**, **Theakston Mild** and up to five regularly-changing guests. It is understandable that it has been the local CAMRA branch Pub of the Year for five years and an ideal place to end the crawl.

Regular buses run from here to Colwyn Bay, Rhos-on-Sea, Rhyl and Llandudno.

Beaumaris

THIS DELIGHTFUL little holiday resort and yachting centre on the Menai Straits has plenty of interest and a handful of fine pubs with a good selection of beers. The nearest railway station is six miles away but it is the one with the longest name in Britain: Llanfairpwllgwyngyllgogerychwyrndrobwllllantysiliogogogoch. It is an easy crawl with all five pubs within 400 yards of one another; three are on Castle Street, the main road through the town, and two on its major tributary, Church Street.

The main road from Menai Straits and North Wales (A545) becomes Castle Street and the first pub, at the western end of the town, is the **Liverpool Arms** (1). This is a comfortable, quite large, one-roomed pub close to the straits. It is well divided with alcoves and has a naval theme. There are beers from the **Brains** and **Buckley's** range and good meals are served. Accommodation is available (01248 810362).

Carry on 200 yards and turn left into Church Street and on the right is the timber-framed **George and Dragon** (2) a welcoming local that claims to have been built in 1410 although architectural details suggest a later date – in Elizabethan times perhaps. **Robinson's Best Bitter** and seasonal ales are sold along with good value lunches. A remarkable series of gothic wall paintings came to light in 1970 during renovations and these can be viewed on request.

Higher up the street is the **Sailor's Return** (3) which is predominately a food pub but does sell **Tetley Bitter**, **Boddingtons Bitter**, **Greene King Old Speckled Hen** and occasional guest beers. There is one large room with an open fire in winter and a no-smoking snug for dining. Meals are served at lunchtimes and in the evenings when it can get rather busy. The pub closes in the afternoons. It is well furnished and has a collection of china teapots, antique maps of Cheshire and maritime souvenirs. Bed and breakfast is available (01248 811314).

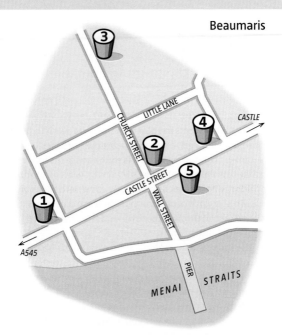

Retrace your steps and turn left into Little Lane and walk
to its end, then turn right into Rating Row and right again
for Castle Street and the **Olde Bull's Head Inn** (4). This is a
Grade II listed building dating from the late 15th century
that was at one time the posting house. It is famed for its
accommodation (01248 810329) with bedrooms named
after Dickensian characters. Charles Dickens was once a
guest here as was Doctor Johnson. The main bar is beamed,
with a large open fire, and is full of interesting artefacts
including a brass water clock. Beers on sale include **Draught
Bass**, **Hancock's HB**, **Worthington's Bitter** and guests and there
are a dozen or so wines by the glass. It has a high reputation
for food with a newly-built brasserie and a rather swanky
restaurant upstairs. The bars are open all day.

Across the street is the **Bulkeley Hotel** (5), an old, well-
established residential hotel (01248 810415) with views
over the Menai Straits and the mountains of Snowdonia.
The bar is open all day and sells **Courage Directors** and

Theakston Cool Cask on the hand pulls. Meals at both lunchtimes and in the evenings have a high reputation.

With a relatively short pub crawl such as this one, and the possibility that you may have stayed overnight in the town, then you should take advantage of its other attractions. The 13th-century castle at the end of Castle Street is a must. It was built by Edward I and is unusual in that it was built on a level site in the 'concentric' style with the main structure surrounded by a moat and a curtain wall with towers. It is one of the best examples of medieval military architecture. Also worth a visit are the Museum of Childhood Memories, also in Castle Street, and the Gaol and Courthouse Museum at the west end of the town in Gaol Street.

The Mumbles Mile

THE SEASIDE VILLAGE OF MUMBLES lies five miles along the coast from the city of Swansea and used to be reached on the famous Mumbles Railway. This was the first passenger railway in the world taking visitors in horse-drawn cars from as early as 1807. Sadly it closed in 1960 but you can now walk or cycle along the scenic route next to the sea shore or simply catch a bus.

Mumbles has a history dating back to Roman times and Oystermouth Castle is a prominent local landmark. Mumbles was well-known in the 19th century for oyster fishing and the quarrying of its limestone cliffs. When the famous diarist, the Reverend Francis Kilvert, visited Mumbles in 1872 he wrote that 'the great fleet of oyster boats was coming in round the lighthouse point with every shade of white and amber sails gay in the afternoon sun'.

Sadly the oysters are no longer plentiful, but the parish is still known as Oystermouth and our tour starts in Oystermouth Square where the original railway terminus was. This is also the start of the famous, or some say infamous, Mumbles Mile – a pub crawl that has been popular for at least a century. Your pub crawl is going to be a little more discriminating than the traditional seafront crawl and you will explore some interesting back-street pubs as well as some of those on the Mile itself.

Our starting point is the well-known **White Rose** (1) a busy pub near the waterfront and castle in a prominent position on the corner of Newton Road. The pub has long been known as a **Bass** and **Worthington's** house and caters for a wide range of customers with reasonably-priced food menus. It is a large and busy pub and, as it is generally reckoned to be the starting point of the Mumbles Mile, it can be packed with young people, especially at weekends.

Move from the White Rose along the front and turn right into Dunns Lane and then left into Park Street, to

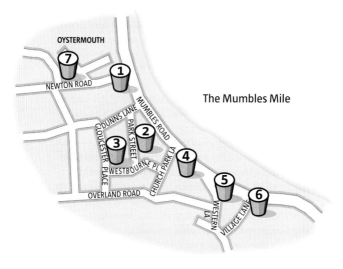

The Mumbles Mile

discover one of Mumbles' best-kept secrets, the **Park Inn** (2). This is a perennial back-street local where conversation is the order of the day. The beer range features **Swansea Three Cliffs Gold**, **Worthington's Bitter** and guest beers from local brewers. A splendid collection of pump clips decorates the bar. The Park is popular with locals and visitors alike, and the meals are all home-cooked, with daily specials available. It has twice been Swansea CAMRA Pub of the Year and is a must during any visit to the area. The street in which the pub is situated is a regular winner of the Mumbles in Bloom competition.

We next move around the corner into Westbourne Place and the **Victoria Inn** (3), another pleasant watering-hole tucked away from the crowds on the seafront. The Vic is a lovely old back-street corner local dating from the mid-19th century as the name implies. The pub has been tastefully renovated, retaining the stained-glass windows and making a feature of the old pub well which was probably the water source in the days when the pub brewed its own beer. The pub is single-roomed, although there are two distinct areas – the bar area has darts and TV while the other end is a little quieter. It sells **Greene King Old Speckled Hen**, **Worthington's Bitter**, **Draught Bass** (which will be served 'flat' on request) and a guest ale. The pub is open all day.

Our next stop is back on the seafront. Return along Westbourne Place, go along Church Park past the attractive parish church and turn left down Church Park Lane on to the front to find the **Village Inn (4)** on the right. This is a pub with considerable history, dating back to the 18th century, and has been known by many previous names including the New Inn, the Marine Hotel and Vincent's. The present Village Inn is a popular seafront pub, renowned for its **Draught Bass**, which is served direct from the cask. It is frequented by students and business people and is popular for its food. Occasionally it has a variety of live music on offer.

Continuing along the front we come to **Mumbles Rugby Club (5)**, again on the right. This is a friendly little club where temporary membership is always available. The steward is

keen on serving cask ales and always has **Worthington's Bitter** and two guest ales on offer probably from local brewers. Rugby paraphernalia is displayed throughout the club which consists of a friendly bar downstairs with a larger bar upstairs, which is also used for functions.

The final stop is at the **Antelope** (6), which is further along the front towards the famous Mumbles Pier which opened in 1898 when the Mumbles Railway was extended from Oystermouth and many thousands of visitors flocked to the Mumbles, particularly during its heyday in the Edwardian period. The Antelope is a timeless Mumbles pub said to be named after a galleon which frequented Swansea Bay, and the building is little altered since its early days. The beers include **Draught Bass** and **Courage Directors**. The pub was visited by the Swansea-born poet Dylan Thomas in his younger days:

> *'Oh as I was young and easy in the mercy of his means,*
> *Time held me green and dying*
> *Though I sung in my chains like the sea'. (Fernhill)*

If you wish you can continue along the Mumbles Mile to the pier, the home of the Mumbles Lifeboat, and the Pier Hotel which is the recognised finish of the Mumbles Mile. And if you happen to be in the area on the Thursday, Friday or Saturday before the August Bank Holiday then visit the popular Mumbles Beer Festival at the **Ostreme Hall** (7). The festival is an important part of the Mumbles social calendar and features more than 50 real ales and ciders.

Rugby and beer

RUGBY AND BEER go pint in hand in Wales. But in the 19th century the brewer's influence reached beyond the bar to the playing field itself.

In Newport, the game only kicked off when Thomas Phillips of Northampton bought the Dock Road Brewery in 1874. With him came his sons William and Clifford. And with them was a rugby football, "the first ever seen in the town". It had actually been purchased in Rugby and cost 13s 6d. The following year the Newport club was formed after a meeting at the brewery. William Phillips was the first captain.

Hancocks went a couple of tries better. Brewery founder William Hancock had ten sons and two of them became international players. Appropriately for a family which had its roots in Somerset before striding over the border to Cardiff, one represented England and the other Wales.

Frouden "Baby"Hancock became a British lion in 1891 after playing three times for England. Frank, the elder of the two, turned out four times for Wales between 1884 and 1886, but it was while captaining Cardiff that he made his deepest mark on the sport.

He sparked a rugby revolution by becoming the fourth man in the three-quarter line. Using this fresh formation, Cardiff lost only once in the 1886 season. The system soon spread to the Welsh team and then around the world. It still prevails today.

From *Prince of Ales,* Brian Glover

The rest of Europe

FIFTY GREAT PUB CRAWLS only
went beyond mainland Britain to
include two Irish pub crawls – in
Belfast and Dublin. Several users of the
guide suggested that it could spread
out a little further. So from a short list
that also included Paris, Munich and
Boston (Mass.) I chose Amsterdam,
Brussels and Prague mainly because
all three have wonderful pubs and I
was personally more acquainted with
them than the other three cities .

I also felt that at least one of the
islands of Britain deserved the chance
of an entry but there was no obvious
enthusiasm from CAMRA members
except on Jersey where a combined
bus and walking crawl is included.

And finally, as Ireland has so many
fantastic pubs, it has been given
another go with Galway selected by a
short head over Cork and Limerick.

Amsterdam

THERE ARE PLENTY OF GOOD REASONS to visit
Amsterdam and you will know which of them applies
to you. But this guide will concentrate on just one on
the assumption that that is the reason you are
visiting the Netherlands' largest, most interesting
and contrasting city – to sample its drinking cafés.
Cafés are not what the English might expect – such as
genteel teashops – and are more bars than traditional
pubs. They are also called brown cafés, or *kroeg* in
Dutch, from the tobacco stains on the walls and
ceilings, although there are variations in shades of
light brown and white. The ones on this crawl are all
within a mile of the central bus and railway stations
and conveniently arranged for a complete crawl or a
limited one. Any variations are entirely up to you.
Take your time and make it last two or three days and
then go back to the ones you enjoyed most.

All cafés serve snacks and any variations in these
facilities are indicated. Written directions can get
rather long-winded and complicated so invest in the
Falkplan city map from the VVV tourist office and
some shops, and with help from the map in this guide,
find the street and café as indicated. Opening hours
can also get complicated and often change but all the
cafés are open in the evenings until midnight at least –
some open through the day. A copy of Tim Webb's
excellent *Good Beer Guide to Belgium & Holland* is
indispensable.

Visitors to Amsterdam are advised to book
accommodation in advance particular at weekends
and in the summer – try **www.goholland.com**. Public
transport is excellent and a stripkaart for several
journeys on either buses or trams is worth while –
do not attempt to travel without a ticket.

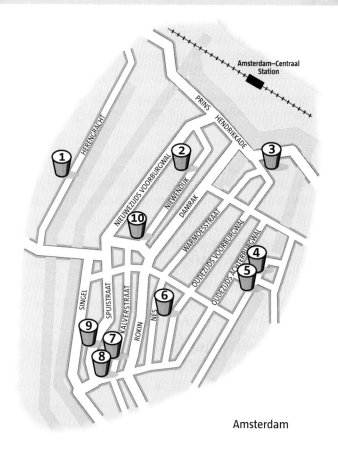

Amsterdam

't Arendsnest (1) Herengracht 90

The Arendsnest opened in 2000 and is unique among the speciality beer cafés in the Netherlands as it serves and stocks only Dutch beers with at least one beer from each Dutch brewery. There are 12 draught beers, six regular and six guest beers, and an ever-increasing range of bottled beers. Since late 2002 under the name 'De Snaterende Arend' (a name derived from the two owners) in cooperation with Dutch breweries they brew their own beers. One, **Nestvlieder**, is permanently available, others as guest beers. The café is

193

in an old canal house looking out over the picturesque Herengracht with a small terrace alongside the canal for summer evenings. The bar with its many brass fittings and the display behind it of not only beers but a large range of jenevers, liqueurs and whiskies is impressive. There are regular tutored beer and whisky tastings. Next door is a Belgian restaurant, *Lieve*, serving good food and a range of Belgian beers.

In de Wildeman (2) Kolksteeg 3 (*Closes Sundays*)

This is certainly one of the best beer cafés in the Netherlands and one of the most famous. It was formerly the premises of an old jenever distillery, the furnishings and fittings of which can still be seen with the old tasting rooms in use as the café. Very much a brown café with 17 beers on draught and over more than 200 bottled including the full range of Trappist beers. Each beer is served in the appropriate glass and if you are unsure what to choose the knowledgeable staff are happy to advise and even give tasters.

Special beers are regularly available and every October there is a Dutch beer week with many beers available on draught and special events such as tastings, quizzes and special meals prepared with beer. There are two bar rooms, a larger one with a raised area at the back and something rarely found in Dutch cafés, a no-smoking room. It also has a no music policy – also rare!

Het Elfde Gebod (3) Zeedijk 5 (*Closes Tuesdays and Wednesdays*)

Quite close to Centraal Station in a small street to the side of the Barbizon Hotel. The area was once notorious and a hang-out of sailors on shore leave, it being the quickest way to reach the red-light district from the station and the harbour. The red-light district may still be there but the area has been cleaned up a lot. On entering the

Eleventh Commandment first appearances, with the brown interior, the carpets on tables and decor are of a traditional Dutch café. Appearances, however, can be deceptive and instead of serving just the customary pils – probably Heineken – it offers seven draught beers and a large range, at the last count more than 50, of bottled beers forming an eclectic mixture and certainly one of the best collections of gueuze beers to be found in the city. It serves bar meals.

Lokaal 't Loosje (4) Nieuwmarkt 32

Next to the eastern edge of the red-light district the café faces on to the large open square that is the Nieuwmarkt. The interior of the main room is tiled from floor to ceiling incorporating several magnificent murals and has a granite-topped bar. The back room is wood-panelled, ornate and chandeliered. Facing the square at the front of the café is a large terrace with an awning should the weather be inclement. There are six draught and some 25 plus bottled beers, generally of an interesting and changing variety. Food is available all day with breakfasts from 9.30 am. On Saturdays there is a farmers' market in the Nieuwmarkt.

De Bekeerde Suster (5) Kloveniersburgwal 6–8

Close to 't Loosje this café was originally the Maximiliaan Amsterdam Brouwhuis which sadly closed due to financial problems. It has now been taken over by the Beiaard group and reopened under the new name but otherwise is very much unchanged, with a large number of rooms on various levels and a restaurant still serving good, inventive food up to 10 pm. On entering the café the first things to meet the eye at the far end of the main bar are the gleaming brewing coppers in the café itself while the rest of the brewery is to be seen through the glass doors at the side of the coppers. The Beiaard group has long wanted its own brewery. Now that it has one the intention is to produce its own house beer for all its cafés and test brews are being produced before a final decision is reached. As well as the main bar there are smaller bars on the upper and lower floors which between them serve a range of ten regularly-changing draught beers and more than 20 bottled beers.

De Brakke Grond (6) Nes 43

The café is part of the complex that forms the Flemish
Cultural Centre with the name De Brakke Grond covering
the whole complex. The café is large and spacious with an
even larger outside terrace in the courtyard that is set back
from the street. Understandably only Belgian beers are
served and those are mainly Flemish. There are six draught
and around 15 bottled beers and a range of Belgian jenevers
and the café is a pleasant and quiet oasis in the centre of
the city. The restaurant is upstairs and open in the evening
offering a full menu, including a special theatre menu,
but food, from snacks to light meals, is served all day
downstairs and on the terrace.

De Pilsner Club (De Engelse Reet) (7) Begijnensteeg 4
(*Closes Sundays*)

De Pilsner Club may be the official name but the café is
better known as De Engelse Reet – the English arse – a name
derived from its proximity to the back of the English Church
in the nearby Beginhof, an enclosed court whose origins
date back to the 14th century. The Beginhof grew over the
years but the court and the houses there, still reserved for
single Christian women, have been maintained in more or
less the original state. The café has a few tables outside;
pleasant if the weather is clement, but most people prefer
to sit inside the one room with its dark and tobacco stained
walls, wooden floor and well worn tables. There are seven
draught beers, including some not so readily available in
Amsterdam, and a range of 12 bottled beers. It is unusual in
the lack of a bar, or at least a traditional bar, with the beer
taps located in a small alcove at the back of the café where
you can go to order. Often regulars will stand and talk to
the owner there, but generally if you sit at a table your
order will soon be taken.

De Beiaard (8) Spui 30

Located by the Singel canal on one of the corners of the Spui,
it has an excellent view over the square. This is a split-level
café, relatively modern in style with two long, narrow rooms
and a semi-enclosed verandah looking towards the nearby

flower market. There are 16 taps for draught beers with a constantly-changing range of guest beers, and 30 or more bottled ones. It is part of the Beiaard group of cafés and every third Monday of the month there is a tutored beer tasting of one brewery's beers, often lead by the brewer. Meals are served up to 9.30 pm. On the Spui, and nearby, there are regular markets for stamps, paintings, curios and books.

Gollem (9) Raamsteeg 4

This was the first Amsterdam café, and one of the Dutch pioneers, to start stocking speciality beers around 30 years ago. Back then of course this meant primarily Belgian, soon joined by beers from Germany and other countries, though it was some time before the Dutch beer revolution started to take off. However, the café does have a special place in the rise and awareness of Dutch beer as it was here that the first Bokbier festivals were held. Though the lighting might be a little more subdued now it is still the same small split-level place it always was; it hardly seems to have changed much over the years and is as welcoming as ever. There are ten draught beers, four more or less regular and six changing guests, and a range of some 200 bottled beers circumnavigating the world.

Belgique (10) Gravenstraat 2

It can be found in a small pedestrian street that is really more of an alley and is close to the Nieuwe Kerk and just off Dam square. This café is small but cosy and in it you enter another world that is seemingly far from the hustle and bustle of city life a stone's throw away. There is a limited amount of seating but the long bar facing the doorway serves eight draught regularly-changing beers and some 35 plus bottled beers. As the name indicates it specializes in Belgian beers and also has a good range of Belgian jenever. Trappist cheeses are included in the snack list.

Brussels

Around the Grand'Place

BRUSSELS IS A GREAT HISTORIC CITY which can justify being visited for its cultural treasures alone. But there is much more. In a political sense it is the capital of Europe and the European Union has its headquarters there. And it is the capital of a nation that has more beer styles than any other. A single pub crawl could not possibly introduce you to all of them but this one does its best and takes you to some characterful and handsome bars in one of the most attractive areas of the city – around the striking Grand'Place.

Anyone visiting Brussels for an extended period – two days or more – is advised to purchase the *Good Beer Guide to Belgium & Holland* by the redoubtable Tim Webb. It will quickly repay its trivial cost. Although Brussels is a bilingual city the most spoken language is French so that is chosen for this crawl where both French and Dutch are in use. You will find English is widely understood particularly where tourism is involved. The transport system of Brussels is excellent and there are many cheap ways of travelling around and they are worth finding out about.

The crawl starts at the Bourse-Beurs (Stock Exchange) tram stop in the Boulevarde Anspach. Go left and left again into rue Henri Maus for **Falstaff** (1) at number 19. It is probably the best-known tavern in the city famous for its Art Nouveau interior, which dates from 1903, and an amazing amount of leaded glass. It was formed from two houses built in 1883. The main bar area sells more than 40 beers mainly from the Interbrew portfolio including Hoegaarden on draught. It has a high reputation for food with a speciality of waffles sold in the afternoons. It used to open 24 hours a day but now shuts down from 5 am to 7 am!

Continue along rue Henri Maus and turn left into rue de Midi which becomes rue de Tabora and on the left down an alley by number 11 is **À la Bécasse** (2) (the woodcock). This is a pleasant 19th-century bar selling draught faro from

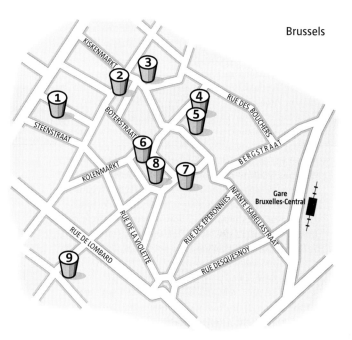

Timmermanns and lambic and kriek from traditional blue-glazed stone jars along with a list of 20 or so other beers, including some from the renowned **Cantillon** brewery in the suburb of Anderlecht. The bar opens from 10 am until midnight and later at weekends and snacks are available until quite late.

Carry on to the crossroads and turn right into the rue Marché aux Herbes and between numbers 6 and 8 is the Impasse aux Cadeaux and **À l'Imaige Nostre Dame** (3) – there is a sign on the main street. This is a classic bar with tiled fireplaces, stained-glass windows and, although brightly lit, has a cosy atmosphere. **Bourgogne de Flandres** and **Timmermanns Blanch-Wit Lambic** are on draught (au fût) with a good list of bottled beers including **Duvel** and **Orval**.

Continue down the rue Marché aux Herbes and turn left into petite rue des Bouchers, which is full of excellent fish restaurants. In an alley off this street the next stop **Toone** (4), is well signed. Its full name is Estaminet Théatre Royal de Toone (Tony's royal theatre tavern) and its address is 6 Impasse Schuddevelde. It is the bar for the puppet theatre with performances every day at 8.30 pm and a matinee on Saturdays at 4.30 pm. Occasional performances are in English. The bar has a small but interesting beer list with **Kwak** and **Hoegaarden** on draught and several Trappist beers and a **Cantillon Gueuze** amongst the bottles. The bars, one of which is no-smoking, open from noon until 2 am each day. Food is available but there is better choice outside.

Back in the rue Marché aux Herbes, opposite the city's main tourist office, at number 56 is **De Bier Tempel** (5) (the beer temple) a speciality beer shop included because it is genuine and reasonable value. On sale are more than 100 beers with its own house brew – **Babelaar**. It also sells presentation packs, glasses, posters and books and it opens from 10 am until 7 pm (9 pm in summer). CAMRA members can obtain a 10 per cent discount on purchases.

Cross the road and walk down rue Chair et Pain into the Grand'Place, turn right and on the right is **Le Roy d'Espagne** (6) (the King of Spain) one of the most impressive houses in this magnificent square. It was built in 1697, renovated a century ago and 50 years later became a café. There are four floors, all worth visiting; in fact a tour before you drink is worth while to allow you to decide where to drink. There is a basement beer cellar; a popular ground-floor room with a circular fireplace, a first-floor bar with wonderful views from its window seats and a traditional pub on the second floor. It is owned by Interbrew which limits the beer list but it does have **Hoegaarden** on draught and the unusual **Hoegaerdse DAS** along with **Rodenbach** and **Duvel** in bottle. It opens most of the day with food from 11 am to 11 pm.

Cross the square to the south-east corner for **Les Brasseurs de la Grand'Place** (7) the first brew-pub to be located in the city in modern times. The brewing vessels are on the immediate left on entering this impressive building which is one of the guild houses – named Au Balance (the scales). There are many separate areas on four floors with two of them no-smoking. The beers are all on draught although bottling is being considered. The regular beers are **Grand'Place Ale**, **Special Grand'Place** and **Brussels Triple** with seasonal specials. All the beers are available in 1.3 litre pitchers and in 2.5 litre columns (La Colonne) with a tap at the bottom. The pub opens from 11 am to midnight and food is served until 11 pm.

Just beyond the pub is a cash machine (hole in the wall) that takes British and American cards. They are not widely found in Belgium except for those that only take local cards.

Move on a few yards to the **Maison des Brasseurs** (8) the headquarters of the Belgium Confederation of Brewers which has a small brewing museum in the basement that is well worth a visit and provides a quiet hour or so from the rush of bars and streets. It costs €3 which includes a drink in a very pleasant old bar. It opens from 10 am to 5 pm except on Sundays.

Your final visit requires a slightly longer walk leaving Grand'Place down rue Charles Buls which becomes rue de l'Étuve and follow the signs for the famous, but rather boring, Manneken Pis (the peeing boy) statue on the corner.

It points, or pees, towards **Le Poechenellekelder** (9) (Punch's cellar) which although full of homage to the boy does however hold more important court to marionettes with thousands of them on display and a puppet theatre upstairs. About 40 beers are on sale including the powerful **Hercule Stout**, **Boon Gueuze**, **Cantillon** beers and several Trappist beers. Basic snacks are served. The bars, including an outdoor terrace, are open from 10 am to midnight and up to 2 am on Fridays and Saturdays but are closed on Mondays.

You can wander back to your starting point through the lanes or take the most direct route by turning right into rue du Chêne and after 100 yards right again on to rue du Marché au Charbon. Go left at rue des Teinturies which leads to the Boulevarde Anspach and the Bourse-Beurs tram stop.

Galway

Ah, they'll say: Padraic's gone again exploring
But now down glens of brightness, O he'll find
An alehouse overflowing with wise Gaelic
That's braced in vigour by the bardic mind.

A tribute to Pádraic Ó Conaire by F R HIGGINS

THE WELL-ESTABLISHED CAPITAL of the west of Ireland is this unspoilt, welcoming, cheerful city with a great cultural life and heritage. It lies close to splendid countryside and sea coast and is a perfect spot to tour from with beautiful Connemara on its doorstep to the west and the Burren a few miles to the south. The centre of Galway remains much as it was in the late 19th century with narrow lanes, high buildings and the pleasant open Eyre Square at its centre with its statue of the poet Pádraic Ó Conaire. And there are many historic memories – the Spanish Arch by the harbour is a reminder of trading with Spain in the 16th century. Access to the three Aran Islands is easy by air and ferry. Galway is linked to Dublin by air, express rail and good roads.

The pub crawl starts at the railway station in the centre of the city. To the right of the front of the railway station in Forster Street is **Rabbitt's (1)**, a rather splendid, classy pub which attracts the business folk of the city and visitors alike. A long bar on the left has high stools and facing this is a series of alcoves which give a degree of privacy to groups of customers. There is also a small off-licensed shop on the left of the door and well provisioned restaurant to the right. All three of the Irish stouts are sold here: **Guinness**, **Beamish** and **Murphy's**, along with an interesting range of bottled beers both locally and from the continent. There are also some excellent single malt Scotch whiskies and a full portfolio of Irish whiskeys. A piano indicates music and in season that means practically every night. It is a friendly pub with excellent service as befits a business that has been in the same family since it was founded.

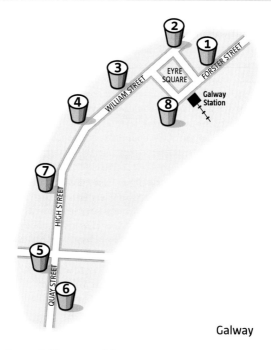

Galway

Cormac Rabbitt opened the premises in 1872 after returning from a spell in California during the gold rush. Originally it was a grocery, then a bar was added, then a restaurant and more lately the off-licence shop.

Move back into Eyre Square for **Tigh Richardson** (2) a large pub on the north-east corner. Tigh is the Irish for pub. The wooden interior has several booths seating four to six people in comparative privacy and there is a large hearth with a turf fire in the middle of one end of the pub. This is a music pub and musicians are most welcome. The food is good value and the stout is fine. A massive collection of car number plates from all over the world are on the walls and thousands of cigarette lighters are attached to the ceiling.

Go into the city centre along William Street where the **Snug** (3) is very easy to miss but is well worth a quick visit. The tiny entrance leads into a narrow pub with very low ceilings and the bar is only about ten feet long and two feet wide and you need to battle through the stool-seated locals to get served although it is all taken with good humour. Once achieved, avoid the thick medieval beams supporting the ceiling and take your place in the giant arc of a stone hearth which dates back to 1292 and enjoy your pint of Guinness.

Further along in High Street is the enigmatic **King's Head** (4) and anyone who can't come out of it without a smile should stop the crawl now. It is stone-floored and the long bar stretches ahead of you ending in a large open space to the left, which culminates in the stage. Do not miss the King and Queen's thrones, but you have to be sharp to get in them. A large selection of beers from around the world is available alongside traditional Irish stouts and other drinks. Upstairs is a second bar and a large seated area that overlooks the stage. Up another floor and there is another bar for more modern music with a DJ on weekend nights. Altogether there are seven separate bars.

Tigh Neachtain (5) in Cross Street is a fine unspoilt pub, more than a century old and once the townhouse of Richard (Trigger) Martin, one-time Member of Parliament for Galway, legendary duellist and the man who founded the Society for the Prevention of Cruelty to Animals. King George IV, who gave the society its Royal prefix nicknamed its founder 'Humanity Dick'. It is in the heart of the city and parking is impossible. The pub's interior is a hotch-potch of small rooms built as pews, cubicles and confessionals. There is a piano, though traditional music is the order of the day here. There are informal sessions on most evenings and folk musicians from all over the world head for Neachtain's. The pub has issued its own album of music recorded in the bar. The walls are covered with theatrical posters and there is a fascinating collection of 'tat' unequalled in any other Galway pub. The bar food is excellent here, reasonably priced and substantial, and there is a restaurant on the first floor. The pub offers a choice of stouts as well as beers from the Biddy Early brewery in neighbouring County Clare.

Move towards the river and the **Quays** (6) is, appropriately, in Quay Street. It is a bit like a Tardis; a tiny façade hides an enormous interior. The small front bar is what is left of the original pub which dates from the 17th century and was called Lydon's. More recently the pub was extended and the lower levels and the rear of the pub are designed in a Spanish style reflecting the fact that for centuries there was extensive trade between Galway and Spain with the nearby Spanish Arch and other architectural features as memories of this. There are several bars in this area with others upstairs where there is also a flourishing restaurant. The original bar, which is popular with local drinkers and has a high reputation for its stout, holds one of the oldest licences in Ireland and it is easy to believe in its longevity. Music is a big feature of the Quays with sessions of traditional Irish, jazz and blues and many famous names have appeared here.

Returning towards the city centre and back in High Street is **Murphy's** (7). Murphy's Law is: 'if something can go wrong, it will go wrong'. But how wrong can such a law be here for little ever seems to go wrong in this the most traditional of Galway pubs. To call it unspoilt is to undermine it, for what few changes there have been since Philip Murphy bought it in 1931 have been for the better. It is basic, friendly, bustling and most welcoming. At one time the pub sold groceries, a regular practice which now, sadly, appears to be vanishing particularly in urban areas but the lack of it does not detract from the atmosphere of this wonderful pub. Murphy's Law is well displayed on the pub walls along with a number of other laws and dictums one of which is: 'celibacy is not hereditary.'

Return to Eyre Square and on the bottom corner is **Foxes Pub** (8) just two minutes' walk from the railway station and perfect for a quick drink before jumping back on to the train. It is very cosy, warm and welcoming with a tiny dance floor. Music is mixed but mainly traditional and there are lots of seats. It sells a wide selection of beers and ciders.

Jersey
St Aubin, Portelet and Ouaisne

JERSEY IS THE LARGEST of the Channel Islands and one of the most popular holiday resorts in the British Isles. You can travel there by ferry from England, France and Guernsey and by air from a dozen or so mainland airports. It has a temperate climate, beautiful scenery in particular on its coastline, and many sites of archaeological, historic and cultural interest. The administrative centre, St Helier, has plenty of accommodation and is a good centre to make journeys to all parts of the island.

This pub crawl is based around the pretty bays of south-west Jersey and does involve climbing a couple of steep hills. It starts however by taking a bus from St Helier, where most people stay and is the terminus for all buses to St Aubin.

Along the harbour side at St Aubin is the **Old Court House** (1). The pub has all the granite character you would expect of a 15th-century Jersey merchant house and on a sunny day when the tide is in the view of the harbour is one you will

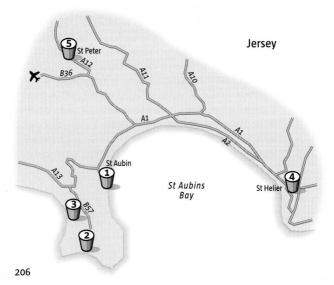

long remember. Scholars of Bergerac will recognise the bay window! The pub has a number of different rooms inside, all full of character, and an award-winning restaurant upstairs. It is very popular with the trendy set and the courtyard may be packed on a summer's evening but don't let that put you off. There are always a couple of real ales on offer with **Marston's Pedigree** as a regular and a guest beer or two. It opens all day and accommodation is available (01534 746433).

Turn right on leaving and walk up the hill. It is very steep so take your time, but it does take you through a picturesque row of houses past the Somerville Hotel and up Ghost Hill, so called because of the graveyard at the top. Legend has it that a cart containing coffins lost its load and that the owners of the wretched bodies which rolled down the hill revisit the hill on dark nights. One benefit of climbing a steep hill such as this (and this is worth repeating to yourself with each step) is the magnificent view you get when you reach the top. Be sure to turn round to see it.

At the end of the road, about half a mile after it has flattened out, turn left and head for Portelet Bay where facilities at the **Portelet Inn** (2) will help revive you. This is a classic 17th-century Jersey farmhouse in pink granite and it enjoys spectacular views over the bay. It is one of Jersey's most popular pubs, particularly with tourists, who can then tackle the long path down to the beach. It serves good food, including Sunday lunches and snacks all day in large well laid out indoor and outdoor eating areas including a no-smoking family room. It opens all day and there are bars both upstairs and downstairs serving hand pulled **Boddingtons Bitter**, **Courage Directors** and guest beers. Look out for the traditional granite cider press in the front courtyard – a common feature of Jersey farmhouses.

After a restful afternoon viewing the bay, walk back the way you came, but turn down to Ouaisne on the left which is signposted. The road is cool and leafy and ends at the **Old Smugglers Inn** (3) in what was once a row of fishermen's cottages. Here is more granite, more character and more excellent food inside what is one of Jersey's few free houses. Unlike most of the pubs on the island there is a more interesting range of beers here, with **Draught Bass** as a regular and often guests from the **Ringwood Brewery**. It opens all day and is highly regarded by local CAMRA members. A walk along the beach at Ouaisne Bay is well worth while, especially if the sun is setting.

To catch a bus back to St Helier, walk back up the hill out of the bay and turn left at the top. Follow the road for about half a mile and it takes you to the main road where there is a bus stop on the other side of the road. If you take the bus all the way to the bus station at the Weighbridge, you are ideally positioned to finish your crawl in the **Lamplighter** (4), an institution on the Jersey real ale scene. Unashamedly a drinkers' pub, the single bar is full of character and of characters. It is the only gaslit pub in Jersey and has a range of five real ales – **Draught Bass**, **Boddingtons Bitter**, **Courage Directors**, **Theakston Old Peculier** and a guest ale together with real cider. It has been CAMRA Jersey's Pub of the Year on several occasions in recognition of consistently good beer quality and choice. It opens all day and bar food is served at lunchtimes. Take time to look at the top of the pub from the outside.

You are quite likely to be staying on the island for more than one day so you may be interested in visiting Jersey's only brewery which is in St Peter about five miles from St Helier and served by buses. The **Star and Tipsy Toad Brewery** (5) was refurbished recently and the Star pub is smart and bright with a variety of drinking and dining areas surrounding a central bar which sports a stained-glass roof. All the **Tipsy Toad** beers are sold here and while demand often outstrips supply, you can usually rely on the award-winning **Jimmy's Bitter** being on tap and maybe a guest ale. Tours of the brewery are available on request but it may be advisable to ring in advance (01534 485556). The pub opens all day from 11 am and serves lunches and evening meals, except on Sundays when there is no food.

Prague

Though the latitude's rather uncertain,
And the longitude also is vague,
The persons I pity, who know not the city,
The beautiful city of Prague.   WILLIAM JEFFREY PROWSE

THE CZECHS are the world's greatest beer drinkers so we can expect them to know something about the drink and how to make it. And we, the visitors, should expect to find good quality beers and it goes without saying that we do. Prague is now amongst the top ten visited cities in Europe and deservedly so for it has so much to offer beyond its beer credentials. It is a beautiful city – the 'golden' city – and it is to be expected that a visit there would not simply be for this pub crawl. A good guide book and street map are recommended. The unit of currency is the koruna – the crown – abbreviated to kc and in summer, 2003, the rate of exchange was about 43 kcs to the pound or 2.3p to the kc.

A useful tip about drinking is that you pay for everything when you leave the bar. Buying a round is not a general practice in the Czech Republic (or indeed in most of central and eastern Europe) where the custom is for the waiter to mark what drinks you have on a pad or even the back of a beer mat and present your party with a bill at the end of your visit. Generally speaking you can trust waiters not to overcharge and it can sometimes be the case that they forget a round – but not often! And please remember that here closing time does not mean last orders; it is the time the door is locked and the staff are on the way home, so last orders should be regarded as at least half an hour earlier.

The Czechs use a system of measuring alcohol called Balling which was originally in degrees but now appears to be shown with a percentage mark (%) which is confusing when compared with the system used in western Europe of alcohol by volume (abv). In this crawl the Balling system is

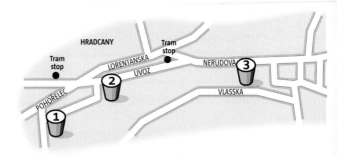

used in its original form of degrees (°). It is difficult to make comparisons but some examples are Balling 10° – abv 3.8%, Balling 12° – abv 5%.

Public transport in Prague is excellent and cheap but you cannot buy tickets on trams; they should be bought at metro stations, tobacco and newspaper kiosks and in some places from machines. At the time of writing a single journey ticket costs 8 kcs (about 18p), and there are 1-day, 3-day and 7-day unlimited travel tickets. Stamp the ticket in the machine on the tram, bus or metro station the first time you use it. Travel without a valid stamped ticket can incur a fine from a plain-clothes inspector. It is worth mentioning that pickpockets "work" on the trams so do not let a good holiday mood distract you from taking the usual precautions.

And because this crawl involves quite a steep hill it is best to start off with a tram ride and save your energy. Route 22 to Bílá Hora and 23 to Malovanka provide a combined tram frequency of every five minutes for most of the day although they are less frequent in the evenings and at weekends. Alight at the Pohořelec stop. You can board the 22 or 23 in the city centre at, for example, the Národní třída stop opposite the Tesco department store (28 minutes to Pohořelec) or at Malostranská station on the metro line A (7 minutes from Pohořelec). From Vacslavske namesti (Wenceslas Square) take the metro line A from Můstek station to Malostranská.

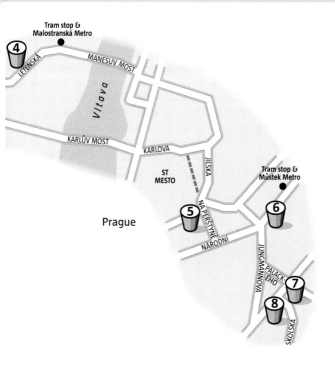

When you get off the tram, continue in the same direction, across the square, then up the hill to the right, about 100 yards. Go through the arch into the grounds of the Strahov monastery of the Premonstratensian Order. After about another 100 yards, on the left and past a gallery building, is the **Klášterní pivovar** (1) (the Monastery Brewery). Do not be diverted by signs for another restaurant. The courtyard here is a pleasant place to sit in fine weather, and has about 20 tables, and inside there are a few more tables and a view of the brewing equipment. Two beers are brewed regularly, a pale 12° beer and a dark 14°, both under the name of **Svatý Norbert** (Saint Norbert). A minor irritant is that they are served in 0.4 litre glasses instead of the 0.5 litre, that is usual in the Czech Republic. The glasses are an unusual shape, being almost like a globe. The price is also closer to western European prices than usual, at 49 crowns (about £1.10). Jantar is advertised on the gate but seems to be no longer available. Budvar is also served. The beer is good, the service friendly and attentive, and the staff can speak English. From outside there is also a really spectacular view over the river.

When leaving, go down the hill, not back to the tram stop but along the street called Pohořelec for about 200 yards, and then fork left. On the right the pavement runs through sets of arches. Between the first and second arch, opposite Loretanské náměstí (Loretto Square) is the next stop, **U černého vola** (2) (The Black Ox). There are no hanging signs outside, few people without a knowledge of Czech would realise it is a pub, it is easy to walk past without noticing it and so we have, in effect, right in the main tourist area, a traditional Czech pub with no tourists. It has been a pub for about 40 years, though the building is older, and the present licensee frequented it when it was a youth club. Everything about it exudes Czech tradition, even the opening hours of 10 am to 10 pm – the usual closing time in the Communist days. There is only one room and it is busy most of the time, so be prepared to share the heavy dark wooden tables with others or you can also stand at the bar and pay direct. The walls are white, adorned with coats-of-arms of old Czech noble families. There are no full meals, only snacks. There are two beers, pale and dark, both from the brewery at **Velké Popovice**, south-east of Prague, now owned by Pilsner Urquell, itself a subsidiary of South African Breweries. Both cost a more traditional Czech price of 21 kcs (about 48p). They are marketed under the name of **Kozel** (Billy-Goat). There are three certificates on the pub wall: one is from a society of enthusiasts of the pub that was formed a few years ago to campaign against rumours that it was to be sold and altered unsympathetically; one is a well-kept-beer certificate from the brewery; and one is a 'Pub-of-Dreams' certificate from the beer drinkers' monthly paper *Pivní Kurýr* (Beer Courier).

To find the next pub it is essential to follow directions precisely. Turn right out of the door and go down past the ornamental light in the middle of the square. About 100 yards further, by a sign on the right that in old-fashioned script says "Hostinec ve Staré Radnici AD 1605" the road kinks and narrows and there are steps down to the right. The sign means "Pub in the Old Town Hall" and Zlatopramen 11° beer is advertised at a clear rip-off price of 80 crowns (£1.84). Go down these steps, which are called Radnické schody (Town Hall Steps) and continue down a street called Nerudova. Czech buildings usually have two numbers, one being a sequential number for postal purposes and the other a land registry number. At the building 13/250 there is an archway into an arcade-like layout on the right. At this point you can see the Italian Embassy just ahead on the left-hand side of the road; if you have reached the Romanian Embassy (Ambasada României) you have overshot a little. Go through this arch, then on about 20 yards to the bottom of the arcade at the gallery, then right to go behind the gallery. There you will find the **Baráčnická rychta** (3) at Tržiště 23. The name of the pub is difficult to translate precisely, but means the meeting place of a lodge of a kind of society. The main room has wood panelling, a wooden floor, and dining tables. On the wall are pictures of former members, society rules and the lodge standard. There is also a concert room with a stage. The society itself was banned in Communist times, although the pub functioned, and it regrouped after 1989. The standard beers are from **Svijany**, consisting of **Kníže**, a pale 13° at 24 kcs, **Karamel**, a dark 13° at the same price, and **Rytíř**, a pale 12° at 19 kcs. In addition, **Staropramen** 12° beer from the brewery in the Smíchov district of Prague, the largest brewery in the Prague Breweries group, now owned by Interbrew, can be had for 25 kcs, as well as **Pilsner Urquell** at 29 kcs. The food is very good, and opening hours are 12 noon to midnight.

The next stop is easier to find. Return to Nerudova street. Continue down the hill past the Italian, Romanian and other embassies, pass a square on your right. That square is Malostranské náměstí and has a tram stop of the same name (22 and 23 stop there). Unless you have had enough, go straight on following the tram track into the street called Letenská, through the archway nicknamed the 'mouse hole' by tram drivers – it is obvious why – then as the road curves left, on the left is **U svatého Tomáše** (4) (St Thomas's). This is a former monastery, dating from 1352, and had its own brewery in operation until 1951. There is a garden and a cavernous cellar bar, with a souvenir shop. Beers are from the **Ferdinand** brewery at Benešov, south of Prague. This is the same Ferdinand whose assassination in Sarajevo in 1914 is claimed as the excuse for starting the Great War – it was his brewery. There is an 11° dark beer simply called **Ferdinand**, at 26 kcs, and a 13° pale, appropriately called **Sedm kulí** (seven shots) at 28 kcs. In addition, there is **Pilsner Urquell** at 30 kcs and its associated **Gambrinus** 12° at 26 kcs.

To continue the crawl means crossing the famous and historic Charles Bridge (Czech: Karlův most). On leaving turn right, then immediately left into Josefská, then left again opposite the embassy of Serbia and Montenegro. Cross the bridge. On the other side cross the road and tram tracks into a semi-pedestrian street called Karlova. At the fork in the street by a wine bar called *U zlaté studni* take the right fork then at the next corner turn right into Husova. This continues into Na Perštyně. On the right-hand side, at number 7, with Tesco in sight ahead, is **U Medvídků** (5). It is easy to miss the door, but go in and turn right. This is another traditional Czech pub, with light wooden panelling, and is a rare outlet for **Budvar** in Prague (at 24 kcs), and it also sells a dark 12° beer called **Granát** from **Černá Hora** in Moravia, at the same price. They also sell bottles of **Bud 16° Super Strong** at 30 kcs for 0.33l – it is genuine Czech beer – not American! It opens from 11 am to 11 pm.

On leaving, continue towards Tesco, but at the end of the street turn left into Národní. When you reach a metro entrance and a sign for a pedestrian zone there is a pedestrianised street ahead. On your right you will see the Austrian Cultural Forum. You need to go to the far left of

U Medvídků, Na Perštyně 7

Although interpreted as 'The Little Bears' – and there is an etching above the entrance – it is possibly named after a family that owned it at one time. This tavern has been a brewery, a music hall and a haunt of leading city officials, artists and writers – the writer Jiří Marek set one of his detective stories in it. And Vaclav Havel celebrated there in 1975 after the performance of one of his plays, *The Beggar's Opera,* by an amateur company. He wryly commented on the closeness of the police station.

It is an ancient building and brewing took place there as early as 1438. The small entrance belies the size of the place with a large main room and a smaller snug behind and a graceful courtyard for summer drinking. Beers are served from an enormous tap in front of the kitchen and an old beer wagon stands in the centre of the main bar. Beer glasses are placed on ceramic coasters, an old Czech tradition rarely seen today.

this building into a square parallel to the pedestrianised street, and in Jungmannovo náměstí at 15/16, is **U Pinkasů** (6), recently reopened after extensive renovation. The pub takes its name from the Pinkas family who once owned it. It is on three levels, including a cellar bar that opens from 4 pm to 4 am, and the ground floor and the first floor being open from 11 am to 10 pm. For many years its repute has been based on its **Pilsner Urquell**, at 27 kcs, which is also sold under its Czech name of **Plzeňský Prazdroj**. There is also another chance to drink dark **Kozel** from **Velké Popovice** at the same price.

Retrace your steps to the metro entrance, turn left into Jungmannova, next left into Palackého, and you will come to the tram track. This is Vodičkova; turn right, and on the left at 26 is the **Branický sklípek** (7) (Braník Cellar). On the left is a large room for eating, on the right a small room for drinking. They sell 10° and 12° pale beers from **Braník** which is part of Prague Breweries, dark 11° **Staropramen** from the **Smíchov** brewery of the same group, all three at 20 kcs, and also a stout-like beer called **Kelt**.

Finally, on the same side of the road, three doors away is the **Novoměstský pivovar** (8) (New Town Brewery), a home-brew pub that opened in 1994. It is reached from the tram stop along a long passage through a shopping arcade and could be easily missed. They sell unfiltered 11° beers, in dark and pale forms. There are corridors and alcoves and with ten different rooms in all it can be quite an intimate place for a private group. Opening hours are officially 8 am to 11.30 pm from Mondays to Fridays, 11.30 am to 11.30 pm on Saturdays and 12 noon to 10 pm on Sundays, but here last orders an hour before closing time might be a wise assumption. Beer is sold to take away and there is a souvenir shop.

This is probably enough for most people. At the end you are very central – Vacslavske namesti (Wenceslas Square) is a short distance away – go out of the pub, turn right, and follow the tram tracks for about 300 yards – and with it the metro station at Můstek, where two lines meet. You will have had the chance to try about 20 different beers from ten different breweries, including two pub-breweries and including two regional breweries whose products are unlikely to be found elsewhere in Prague.

A virtual pub crawl – soap pubs

THE EDITOR *who suffers from osteoarthritis in both knees and finds it difficult to walk very far decided to take a tour of the pubs of your favourite soap operas from his armchair.*

For several years I worked in the press office of the Great British Beer Festival. By Friday at one of the four Leeds-based festivals most of our work was done and so the team spent time on some rudimentary market research. We set out to find which of the four soap opera pubs the drinkers liked best, and why.

Their choice was from the Woolpack in what was then called *Emmerdale Farm*, the Rovers Return in *Coronation Street*, the Queen Vic in *EastEnders* and the only radio pub, the Bull at Ambridge in *The Archers*. Few chose the Bull but one man was quite determined in his support for what was the oldest of the four in broadcasting terms. And what was it that appealed to him most? 'The decor', he replied.

At the time I was compiling a guide called *The Best Pubs in Yorkshire* and, with the approval of the managing editor, decided to include the Woolpack in Beckingdale (as the village was then called) as a spoof entry. It was all for a bit of fun.

The cartographer was our good friend David Perrott, who has drawn the maps for this guide. He lives in wild, west Wales and late one night – way after midnight – just before going to the final press stage, he phoned me in obvious concern. 'Where the blankety-blank is Beckingdale?' he screamed down the phone. 'I've checked every map of Yorkshire and I can't find it anywhere.' I calmed him down and told him it was a spoof entry and apologised for not letting him in on the joke. Off he went to his bed reasonably satisfied.

The following morning it seemed to me that here was an opportunity not to be missed. I telephoned a fellow journalist who worked in the Yorkshire Television press office and related the tale. He was delighted and immediately sent out a media release. It was picked up at once particularly by the tabloids and the local papers, and both the programme and the book got plenty of publicity. One headline was 'The pub that never was.'

So you have been warned. The four pubs that follow are virtual pubs – they don't exist in the real world only in that of the soaps. Though I can say that I have been in two of them and was actually served a drink in the Woolpack, but that's another story.

Hosts Sid and Jolene Perks invite you to the **Bull**, at Ambridge, lost somewhere in the Hereford, Gloucester, Worcester triangle in *The Archers* (BBC Radio 4 Mondays to Fridays at 7 pm with an omnibus edition on Sundays at 10 am). This is a real old-fashioned English free house serving excellent **Shires** ales. Traditional darts and dominoes are played in the public bar and in the cosy Ploughman's bar food is always available. There are also good value meals in the family restaurant. The pub opens at 10 am for coffee and the newspapers. The first-floor function room features line dancing with Jolene on Tuesdays and The Bull Upstairs from Thursdays to Saturdays is for the younger set, with CD juke box, occasional bands and DJs. It is available for private functions at other times. Outside there is plenty of car parking, a beer garden with Eccles the peacock and a boules piste with equipment available from behind the bar. Look for the half-timbered building just off the Village Green. The landlord is the manager of the Ambridge cricket team that has its headquarters here. Website: www.bbc.co.uk/radio4/archers

The **Rovers Return** in Coronation Street, Weatherfield, Greater Manchester is a predominate scene in the programme *Coronation Street* (ITV 1 on Sundays, Mondays, Wednesdays and Fridays at 7.30 pm, although times change occasionally, with repeats on ITV 2 later the same evening), Fred Elliot is the latest licensee with Shelley as his manager. It is a brick-built, terrace end pub built in 1902 by the Newton and Ridley brewery and was originally named after Lieutenant Philip Ridley following his return from the Boer War. It was originally spelled 'Rover's' but Ridley dropped the apostrophe to dedicate it to all local men who served in the war. Up to the mid-eighties it had a tiny snug usually the preserve of elderly ladies but this vanished during a refurbishment that followed a fire. It is now open-plan with an L-shaped bar and a dartboard where the snug used to be. There is a mystery: spot the gents toilets in the top right-hand corner and explain how they come to share the kitchen of Ken Barlow's house next door. It sells beers from **Newton and Ridley** the local brewery, **John Willy Lees** and **Boddingtons**. Lunches are served with hot-pots prepared by Betty Turpin, the longest-serving member of the staff, being much in demand although because Elliot is also a butcher his pies tend to be promoted more. Always busy, usually with the same drinkers. Find out more on www.itv.co.uk/coronationstreet

The **Queen Victoria** stands on the corner of the main entrance to Albert Square in Walford, East London. The pub takes its place in the *EastEnders* programme (BBC 1 on most weekdays at either 7.30 pm or 8 pm). It is brick-built with a quite elaborate façade and it dates from the 1870s and was obviously named after the reigning Queen. The present guvnor is the fast-talking Alfie Moon. There is a single long bar serving hand pulled ales from local breweries and the lunchtime food is hearty but pretty basic. The decor has not changed much over the years and includes a handsome Victorian fireplace. This is a locals' pub with a definite east end bias including a piano for occasional singalongs. Easy to find on www.bbc.co.uk/eastenders

Your final stop is at the **Woolpack** in the centre of Emmerdale village in the Yorkshire Dales and the principal meeting place for the characters in *Emmerdale* (ITV 1 on five nights a week, usually Mondays to Fridays at 7 pm with repeats on the following day). It is a handsome country pub dating from around 1850. It belongs to the **Ephraim Monk** brewery in north Yorkshire that was established in 1778 making it the second oldest brewery in the county. There is just one large room with separate areas and it is reasonably well-appointed. The tables on the forecourt are well used in summer. On the hand pumps are **Monk's Bitter** and **Old Ranter** and recently **Black Sheep** beers have appeared, perhaps as guests. Meals are served at lunchtimes and in the evenings and they seem popular although the credentials of the chef, Marlon Dingle, are suspect, he being self taught in a couple of months. The joint licensees are the feisty Diane Blackstock and her Australian partner (in the Dales?) Louise Appleton. Keep up with the action on **www.emmerdale.co.uk**

Funny things happen in soap pubs. A good friend of mine is a bit part actor and I can swear that I saw him in the bar of the Woolpack at 7.25 one evening and then ten minutes later in the Rovers Return. How did he get there? Certainly not by the M62.

Index of places

What is CAMRA?

CAMRA is an independent, voluntary, consumer organisation. Membership is open to all individuals, but corporate entities such as breweries and pubs are not members. CAMRA is governed by a voluntary, unpaid, national executive, elected by the membership. There is a small professional staff of eighteen responsible for central campaigning, research, administration of membership, sales and so forth.

How is CAMRA financed?
CAMRA is financed through membership subscriptions, sales of products such as books and sweatshirts, and from the proceeds of beer festivals. It receives no funding from the brewing industry other than a limited amount of advertising in the monthly newspaper *What's Brewing*.

CAMRA's objectives
CAMRA's mission is to act as champion of the consumer in relation to the UK and European beer and drinks industry. It aims to:

- Maintain consumer rights
- Promote quality, choice and value for money
- Support the public house as a focus of community life
- Campaign for greater appreciation of traditional beers, ciders and perries as part of national heritage and culture
- Seek improvements in all licensed premises and throughout the brewing industry
- CAMRA also seeks to promote real cider and perry through a sub-organisation called APPLE. Like ale, these are traditional British drinks and like ale, the traditional product is very different from the 'dead' version.

Campaigning
While CAMRA is a single industry group, it has a very wide area of campaigning interests. At present campaigns being actively pursued include the following:

- Improved competition and choice in the brewing industry
- Preserving the British pub and defending licensees from eviction by pub owners
- Seeking a fairer tax system for smaller brewers
- Seeking fuller information about the beer we drink, such as ingredients labelling
- Fighting take-overs and mergers
- Encouraging higher standards of pub design
- Encouraging brewers to produce a wide range of beer styles such as porter, mild and stout, in addition to their bitters.

Join CAMRA

If you like good beer and good pubs you could be helping to fight to preserve, protect and promote them. CAMRA was set up in the early Seventies to fight against the mass destruction of a part of Britain's heritage. The giant brewers are still pushing through takeovers, mergers and closures of their smaller regional rivals. They are still trying to impose national brands of beer and lager on their customers whether they like it or not, and they are still closing down town and village pubs or converting them into grotesque 'theme' pubs.

CAMRA wants to see genuine free competition in the brewing industry, fair prices, and, above all, a top quality product brewed by local breweries in accordance with local tastes, and served in pubs that maintain the best features of a tradition that goes back centuries.

As a CAMRA member you will be able to enjoy generous discounts on CAMRA books and merchandise and receive the highly-rated monthly newspaper *What's Brewing*. You will be given the CAMRA members' handbook and be able to join in local social events and brewery trips. To join, complete the form below and, if you wish, arrange for direct debit payments by filling in the form overleaf and returning it to CAMRA. To pay by credit card, contact the membership secretary on (01727) 867201. You can also join online at www.camra.org.uk.

Full single UK/EU £16; Joint (two members living at the same address) UK/EU £19;
Single under 26, Student, Disabled, Unemployed, Retired over 60 £9;
Joint retired over 60, Joint under 26 £12; UK/EU Life £192, UK/EU Joint life £228.
Single life retired over 60 £90, Joint life retired over 60 £120.
Full overseas membership £20, Joint overseas membership £23.
Single overseas life £240, Joint overseas life £276. *Please delete as appropriate*:
I/We wish to become members of CAMRA.
I/We agree to abide by the memorandum and articles of association of the company.
I/We enclose a cheque/p.o. for £   (payable to CAMRA Ltd.)

Name(s)

Address

Postcode

Signature(s)

 CAMRA Ltd., 230 Hatfield Road, St Albans, Herts AL1 4LW

Instruction to your Bank or Building Society to pay by Direct Debit

Please fill in the whole form using a ball point pen and send it to:

Campaign for Real Ale Ltd
230 Hatfield Road
St. Albans
Herts
AL1 4LW

Originator's Identification Number

9	2	6	1	2	9

Reference Number

Name of Account Holder(s)

FOR CAMRA OFFICIAL USE ONLY
This is not part of the instruction to your Bank or Building Soc

Membership Number

Name

Postcode

Bank/Building Society account number

Branch Sort Code

Instructions to your Bank or Building Society
Please pay CAMRA Direct Debits from the account
detailed on this instruction subject to the safeguards
assured by the Direct Debit Guarantee. I understand
this instruction may remain with CAMRA and, if so, v
be passed electronically to my Bank/Building Societe

Name and full postal address of your Bank or Building Society

To The Manager	Bank/Building Society
Address	
Postcode	

Signature(s)

Date

Banks and Building Societies may not accept Direct Debit instructions for some types of account

- - - ✂ -

This guarantee should be detached and retained by the Payer.

The Direct Debit Guarantee

- This Guarantee is offered by all Banks and Building Societies that take part in the Direct Debit Schem
  The efficiency and security of the Scheme is monitored and protected by your own Bank or Building So
- If the amounts to be paid or the payment dates change CAMRA will notify you 10 working days in
  advance of your account being debited or as otherwise agreed.
- If an error is made by CAMRA or your Bank or Building Society, you are guaranteed a full and
  immediate refund from your branch of the amount paid.
- You can cancel a Direct Debit at any time by writing to your Bank or Building Society.
  Please also send a copy of your letter to us.